Legitimacy and

■ POLITICAL DYNAMICS OF THE EU SERIES ■

Series Editors:
**PROFESSOR KENNETH DYSON AND
PROFESSOR KEVIN FEATHERSTONE**

The Common Foreign Security Policy of the EU
DAVID ALLEN

Franco-German Relations
ALISTAIR COLE

A Multi-Speed European Integration Process: Between Hegemony and Dependency?
KEVIN FEATHERSTONE

The Single European Market
ALAN BUTT PHILIP

Technocracy
CLAUDIO M. RADAELLI

European Social Policy
MARTIN RHODES

Legitimacy and the EU

DAVID BEETHAM AND CHRISTOPHER LORD

LONGMAN
London and New York

Addison Wesley Longman Limited
Edinburgh Gate
Harlow
Essex CM20 2JE
United Kingdom
and Associated Companies throughout the world

*Published in the United States of America
by Addison Wesley Longman, New York*

First published 1998

ISBN 0 582 30489 X

British Library Cataloguing-in-Publication Data

A catalogue record for this book is available from the British Library

Library of Congress Cataloging-in-Publication Data

A catalog record for this book is available from the Library of Congress

Set by 35 in 10/12 Sabon
Printed in Malaysia, PP

Contents

Series Editors' Preface

The decade of the 1990s has been associated with a series of key changes in Europe that have raised major issues for European integration at the start of the new millenium. Some of these changes – the end of the Communist regimes in Eastern Europe, the collapse of the Soviet Union, and German unification – have occurred, of course, outwith the established processes of the European Union. But, in parallel to these changes, the European Union has itself embarked on a major project of both 'widening' and 'deepening', with its agenda dominated by the policies of enlargement and of Economic and Monetary Union. The 'deepening' of the integration process has, in turn, provoked a public backlash in some member states of the EU, as evidenced in the ratification debates on the Maastricht and Amsterdam treaties. In short, the EU faces a period of external challenge, internal reform, and public uncertainty of an unprecedented magnitude.

With this in mind, the emphasis of this new series is very much on the dynamics of the European Union. Together, each of the volumes will analyse and reflect on the implications of such changes for the European integration process in the next decade.

The series also seeks to encourage undergraduate students to reflect theoretically on the implications of these changes. Just how adequate are different analytic frameworks for understanding what is happening in a given area of integration? The series will usefully complement more descriptive and institutionally-based accounts of European integration. At the same time the editors avoid imposing a single theoretical approach on what they recognize to be a wide-range of varying experiences across different areas.

In addition to encouraging theoretical reflection, the series seeks to give a strong empirically-grounded content to each volume in the form of brief case studies, which are designed to illustrate important aspects of the phenomenon under investigation. These case studies focus in particular on the theme of power: of where power lies and of how it is exercised.

Finally, the series encourages authors to reflect on scenarios for development in the policy field or issue area with which they are concerned. In this way, the theoretical and empirical foci of the volumes are brought together.

It is appropriate that the first volume of the series should be about legitimacy and the EU. In the wake of the Danish referendum of 1992 this issue has taken on added significance. The negotiations leading to the Amsterdam Treaty of 1997 focused, in particular, on institutional reform and the promotion of citizenship rights. The transition to Economic and Monetary Union in 1999 raises questions about the accountability of monetary policy and the political direction of economic policy. The issue of legitimacy is central to an EU that is in a period of flux. It is linked to a range of policy debates. Yet, it is a subject that has been tratitionally neglected by the literature on the EU. The volume by David Beetham and Christopher Lord thus fills an important gap in our understanding of legitimacy in the context of the European Union

Professor Kenneth Dyson
Professor Kevin Featherstone
University of Bradford

CHAPTER ONE

Analysing legitimacy in the EU

From at least the time of the ancient Greeks onwards political philosophers have debated about what it is that makes government
rightful or legitimate, and what criteria have to be met if those
subject to political authority are to have an obligation to obey
it (Pateman, 1985; Horton, 1992). 'The strongest is never strong
enough to be master,' wrote Rousseau, 'unless he transforms
strength into right and obedience into duty' (Rousseau, 1963: 6).
But what exactly is it that creates 'right' and 'duty'? Philosophi-
cal arguments in Western political theory about this key issue have
rarely been a merely academic matter; they have usually been
symptomatic of some profound dilemma or crisis of political order,
and have reflected much wider debates and disagreements about
its legitimacy within society itself. The rich tradition of normative
political theorising, in other words, which we read now as a self-
contained academic exercise, should properly be seen as a mirror
for real and live political debate about the grounds, the forms and
the limits of governmental authority in different historical periods.

Since the beginning of the twentieth century this concept of
'legitimacy', of the moral or normative standing of political authority, has been appropriated by social scientists for a rather different
purpose from that of the philosophers. They use it, not so much
to define or justify some ideal criteria for rightful government, but
rather to help analyse and explain the different forms of government that actually exist, and why political order and obedience
are sustained or break down as the case may be (Weber, 1978:
212–15). Thus, through a comparative analysis, different legitimating criteria can be shown to validate and underpin the various
kinds of political system, together with their respective legitimating
institutions and procedures. Likewise the degree of legitimacy of a

political order can help explain the depth of support a government can call on, or its relative vulnerability, when under stress. And the concepts of 'legitimacy deficit' and 'legitimacy crisis' can be used to analyse a growing gulf between principles and practice, or between legitimating norms and societal support for them, which heralds a process of political upheaval, renewal or transition (Habermas, 1976: 1–8).

The subject of this volume, *Legitimacy and the European Union*, calls for exploration under both of these modes of analysis, the normative and the analytical. On the one hand, the authority and scope of EU institutions is a subject of considerable political controversy in many member countries; and associated with this controversy are very different conceptions of political identity, of sovereignty and of the conditions for effective and accountable government, and very different ideals for the kind of Europe that might evolve in the future. On the other hand, these essentially normative concerns are also reflected in the analytical disputes between political scientists: about what kind of political phenomenon the EU is, or is on the way to becoming; about what the appropriate criteria of legitimacy are for the institutions of the EU and for its regulative and legislative authority; about whether there is a 'legitimacy deficit', and, if so, wherein it lies and how far it matters.

We see a continuum, in other words, between the debates among political actors and publics, and the analytical concerns of political scientists. The legitimacy of the EU is an important subject for normative reflection, because whether and how far the EU's authority is rightful is subject to intense disagreement, with far-reaching implications for political practice. It is also an important subject for political analysis, because the identification of appropriate legitimating criteria, of legitimation procedures and legitimacy 'deficits', will make a necessary contribution to the analysis of the EU as a complex and evolving political system, to identifying the source and extent of its authority, and to understanding the scope and limits of possible change. All these will form the subject of the present volume.

Among the most basic points of disagreement about the EU's legitimacy is whether it should be understood according to the same criteria as those applicable to political authority in the nation state, or quite differently. To answer this key question we have first to be clear about the criteria for political legitimacy at the level of the states which comprise the Union. This will be our starting point. Yet as we shall also argue later, political legitimacy in the European political space has to be understood as a process of interaction between the EU and member state levels. For this reason as well, therefore, we need to begin with the question of what makes authority rightful at the level of the contemporary state.

Once this preliminary work of clarification has been done, we shall then set out our central argument: that the criteria of liberal-democratic legitimacy are indeed appropriate for the EU level, although they may be insufficient on their own, and the institutional forms which embody them may differ from those of individual states. We shall defend this conclusion against counter-arguments, and take a serious look at alternative models of legitimacy that have been proposed for the EU, such as that of international institutions, on the one hand, and bureaucratic or technocratic legitimacy, on the other. In the second part of the book we shall use the criteria deriving from liberal democracy – of political identity, popular authorisation and accountability, and key performance criteria – to explore the patterns of interaction between the EU and state levels, and the way these interactions may both reinforce and erode the legitimacy of each.

The concept of legitimacy

What makes political authority rightful or legitimate? At the most general level we can identify a number of criteria which have to be satisfied for any governmental system in any society to be legitimate (Beetham, 1991: 15–20). Three different dimensions can be distinguished. Political authority is legitimate, we can say, to the extent that:

1 it is acquired and exercised according to established rules (legality)
2 the rules are justifiable according to socially accepted beliefs about (i) the rightful source of authority, and (ii) the proper ends and standards of government (normative justifiability)
3 positions of authority are confirmed by the express consent or affirmation of appropriate subordinates, and by recognition from other legitimate authorities (legitimation).

The first of these levels is that of rules; the second that of justifications grounded in beliefs; the third that of acts of consent or recognition. The three levels are not alternatives, since all contribute to legitimacy; together they provide the subordinate with moral grounds for compliance or cooperation with authority. Each in turn has its distinctive negative: illegitimacy (breach of the rules); legitimacy deficit (weak justification, contested beliefs); delegitimation (withdrawal of consent or recognition).

How do we arrive at these three analytical dimensions, of rules, normative justifiability and acts of legitimation respectively? By exploring the kinds of answer people give when the rightfulness of authority is challenged. The first step is to show that political power has been acquired and exercised according to the received rules, whether legal or conventional. It is 'lawful'. But that is not enough. We need also to know whether the rules themselves are normatively justifiable according to beliefs current in society. Here two kinds of answer can be given in respect of political authority (Schaar, 1984: 111). The first shows how power derives from a rightful source of authority (divine right, tradition, the people, or whatever), and how this source is reflected in the rules of appointment to office. The second shows how the organisation of power fulfils accepted ends or purposes of government, and meets acceptable standards of rule. Finally, the rightfulness of authority is confirmed by pointing to the acts of affirmation on the part of those subordinates within the society qualified to give it, and by the recognition of other legitimate authorities.

These three dimensions constitute only the most general or abstract framework, the specific content of which has to be 'filled in' for each historical society or political system. They provide a heuristic tool to guide analysis. Is political authority valid according to the rules? The relevant rules have to be specified, their conventional or legal form established, the mode of adjudication appropriate to them determined, and so on. Are the rules justifiable in terms of the beliefs and norms of the particular society, and are these norms relatively uncontested? We need to examine the specific beliefs current in the society about the rightful source of authority, on the one hand, and the proper ends and standards of government, on the other. Are there, finally, actions expressive of consent to authority on the part of those qualified to give it, as well as acknowledgement by other authorities? Who counts as qualified, and what actions count as appropriate, will be determined by the conventions of the given society or system of power, as also what other kinds of authority they are whose recognition has legitimating force.

The overall structure of legitimacy, in other words – its 'heuristic framework' – is a universal one; its specific form is variable according to the historical period, the society in question and the form of political system itself (Beetham, 1991: 21–3). It is a framework that is relevant to both political science and normative philosophy despite their different tasks: in the one, to describe and analyse the legitimating criteria applicable to a specific political order; in the other, to subject them to critical assessment against normatively defensible standards of validity and argument. And if there is a recurrent mistake common to both in their respective analyses of political legitimacy, it is the tendency to reduce the many dimensions of legitimacy to a single one: to legality or procedural regularity alone, to effective performance, or to consent, as the case may be.

The starting point for any analysis of legitimacy, therefore, has to be an acknowledgement of its complexity, and of the full range of factors – rules, normative beliefs, actions and procedures – that contribute to making political authority rightful. The purpose of our threefold schema is to help make this complexity intelligible. It will enable us to identify the distinctive components of liberal-democratic legitimacy, as well as in due course to situate competing accounts of the EU's legitimacy to the one we shall offer.

Legitimacy and liberal democracy

What, then, within this schema, are the defining characteristics of a distinctively liberal-democratic legitimacy? Its typical form of legality or rule-legitimacy, in contrast to political orders whose legality is derived from custom or precedent, from sovereign will or decree, or from sacred texts, can be summed up as the constitutional rule of law: the delimitation of political authority – its scope, duration, mode of appointment and dismissal, etc. – by means of a written constitution, which is adjudicated and enforced by independent courts. This form of legal or procedural legitimacy is one of the distinctively *liberal* features of liberal democracy, and is sustained by a characteristic separation of powers within the state. Political legitimacy in liberal democracy, however, cannot, as some writers have assumed, be exhausted by legal or procedural regularity alone, since the *content* of the constitutional rules, and their conformity to societal beliefs about the valid source of authority and the proper ends and standards of government, can never be treated as irrelevant or inconsequential.

Here come the key normative principles of liberal democracy. On the one hand is the principle of popular sovereignty, and its assumption that the only valid source of political authority lies with the people. From this principle derives the electoral authorisation of government, and the criteria of representation, accountability, and so forth, which comprise the manifestly democratic aspects of liberal democracy's constitutional arrangements. At the same time, however, the legitimating belief that the people constitute the ultimate source of political authority raises acutely the question 'who constitutes the people?', and makes issues of political identity, of territoriality, of inclusion and exclusion, equally crucial for political legitimacy. Considerations of nationhood, in its broadest sense, derive as directly from the principle of popular sovereignty as the criteria for popular authorisation and accountability.

What, on the other hand, of the ends or purposes of government in liberal democracy? These can best be summarised in terms of Lockean rights protection (life, liberty and property, Locke: 1952), complemented by welfare rights and securing the conditions for economic growth, though there is obviously considerable variation of popular expectation within and around this core over time. It is important, however, to distinguish here between the legitimacy of individual governments and of the political order itself. Less important than the success or failure of individual governments for political legitimacy is that the system or organisation of power as such should be seen to facilitate rather than hinder the attainment of its 'performance criteria', and above all should effect the prompt removal of those who have failed or simply grown stale in office. For the latter task liberal democracy's electoral mechanism is particularly effective, since it makes replacement routine, so that failure does not undermine confidence in the system, but allows for political renewal without major upheaval.

That this account of the normative basis of liberal-democratic legitimacy is correct – the people as source of political authority, and rights protection, broadly understood, as the end or purpose of government – can be seen from a glance at two of the most typical founding statements of the liberal democratic era. The US

Declaration of Independence (1776) states that 'to secure these rights – life, liberty and the pursuit of happiness – governments are instituted among men, deriving their just powers from the consent of the governed' (Walker, 1841: 5). The two aspects (the ends of government and the source of political authority) are even more clearly differentiated in the French Declaration of the Rights of Man:

> The end of all political associations is the preservation of the natural and imprescriptible rights of man (sic); and these rights are liberty, property, security and resistance of oppression ... The source of all sovereignty resides essentially in the nation ('the people', 1793 version); nor can any individual or any body of men be entitled to any authority which is not expressly derived from it.
> (Roberts, 1966: 172)

Naturally, the precise reference and scope of these two fundamental principles has been subject to contestation and evolution since that time. Thus who has counted among 'the people' has been a matter of increasing *inclusion*, as the exclusions on the propertyless, women, racial and other minorities, have been successively challenged and eroded. And the definition of rights protection has expanded considerably under the pressure of political struggle, to include welfare rights and the general conditions for economic development, indirectly via the market and its regulation if not directly through the state undertaking productive activities on its own account. The standards in both these respects can be expected to be subject to continuing evolution.

Finally there is the distinctive liberal-democratic mode of legitimation through actions and procedures which confirm the acknowledgement of authority by subordinates, and recognition by other authorities. It is often argued that the 'consent of the governed' is the distinctive feature of liberal-democratic legitimacy, and its unique source of obligation to obey political authority (see Pateman, 1985: 81–102; Horton, 1992: 19–50). Yet it is a universal feature of *all* political authority to need to 'bind in' key subordinates through actions and ceremonies which express their consent, their affirmation, or their recognition of the authority: through swearing an oath of allegiance, concluding agreements, according public acclamation, taking part in mass mobilisation in the regime's cause, etc. Such actions publicly confer and confirm legitimacy.

What is distinctive about liberal-democratic legitimation is, first, that the relevant group qualified to confer such recognition is extended to the whole adult population. But, secondly and most importantly, 'consent' is almost wholly subsumed in the *authorisation* of government through the electoral process. Where the governed themselves decide who is to govern them, there is no further need of actions or ceremonies expressive of their consent beyond the electoral procedure for appointment to office. If you authorise someone to act on your behalf, you do not require a separate opportunity to demonstrate consent to their authority. This is the really distinctive feature of liberal democracy compared with all other political systems, that legitimation is subsumed into the procedure for appointment to office, since this is performed by the subordinate themselves. We should thus properly talk of the *popular authorisation* of government, rather than *consent* to it, as the defining characteristic of liberal-democratic legitimation. Insofar as consent has any place at all, it is in popular agreement to constitutional arrangements or revisions in a referendum, which is very different from the electoral authorisation of government. This distinction will be particularly important for understanding legitimacy in the EU.

One final aspect of legitimation needs examination here, and that is the recognition of political authority by other external authorities. A common feature of the contemporary state system is the legitimacy a state derives from recognition by other states. Thus for a new regime to demonstrate to its own population that it has won such international recognition is often an important element in its own internal struggle for legitimacy. This is common to all states, not just liberal-democratic ones. However, there is now an important external support for the internal legitimacy of specifically liberal-democratic regimes in the recognition by, or admission to, the 'family' of liberal-democratic states, and the international support and cooperation that may flow from that recognition. This external support is most powerfully at work in the group of states that make up the European Union, since admission to the EU is itself dependent upon meeting liberal-democratic criteria, and an important part of the EU's project is the safeguarding of these principles among member states. Such recognition is a reciprocal affair, since an important part of the EU's own legitimacy stems from the recognition given to it by the states which comprise it, as will be discussed further later on.

8

Legality

lib-dem form of legality: *constitutional rule of law*

Normative Justifiability

rightful source of political authority		**proper ends and standards of government**
lib-dem: *popular sovereignty*		*rights protection*
definition of the people: identity, inclusion.	criteria for electoral authorisation, representation + accountability	performance criteria procedures to remove failure

Legitimation

lib-dem: *consent subsumed in electoral authorisation; recognition by other legitimate authorities*

Figure 1.1   *Dimensions of Liberal-Democratic Legitimacy*

Thus we have the constitutional rule of law as the distinctive liberal-democratic mode of legality; the principle of popular sovereignty as the source of its political authority, and a broadly construed rights defence (freedom, welfare, security) as the purpose of government; consent subsumed under electoral authorisation, and external recognition and support for its distinctive political arrangements – these are the different elements which together make up liberal-democratic legitimacy in the contemporary world (see Figure 1.1). Our next step is to see whether, and to what extent, these same criteria are applicable to the institutional order and political authority of the European Union. Before that, however, some final points of clarification are in order about the subject of political legitimacy.

When analysing legitimacy, it is important to remember that it is not an all-or-nothing affair, but a matter of degree. The weaker its legitimacy, the less a government can rely on the obedience or support of its subjects when it comes under stress, or requires their particular cooperation to effect its policies. The stability of a political order could be modelled as a relation between the strength of its legitimacy and the force of the pressures to which it is exposed. Thus a regime which relies primarily on performance criteria, as many military regimes do, will be especially vulnerable when performance falters, since it has no valid source of authority, and no rule-governed system for replacing failure. On the other hand, a political system in which there is substantial agreement on the political nation (or disagreement confined to the 'periphery'), and which is secure in its democratic authorisation, representation and accountability, will be able to sustain considerable failure in performance, and even privations for its citizens. Regime crises typically occur when a significant deficit in the source of authority and its validating beliefs is compounded by performance failure, and leads to the active withdrawal of consent on the part of those qualified to give it (Beetham, 1991: 205–42).

Analysts of political legitimacy from Max Weber onwards have argued about whether the recognition or acknowledgement of a regime's legitimacy is only important to the behaviour of its elites or administrative staff, rather than of subjects more widely. Naturally, any regime is particularly dependent on the cooperation of its own officials, and their acknowledgement of its authority is therefore especially important. Yet it is rare in the contemporary world for subjects to be so powerless that a regime can dispense with any wider claim to legitimacy. As long as government depends for the attainment of its policies upon its subjects obeying the laws, paying their taxes, cooperating with its policies and even fighting in its defence, it will require a wider recognition of its legitimacy or moral authority as a condition for effective rule. In other words, the *capacity* of political authorities is not separable from their moral standing among those whose cooperation is required for them to achieve their purposes. One of the key questions about the appropriate form of legitimacy for the EU is whether it has any such direct relationship with citizens of the Union, or only indirectly via the political and administrative officials of its member states.

Finally, the criteria for liberal-democratic legitimacy set out above comprise only what is *typical* for this kind of political system, rather than an exhaustive description of any individual country's legitimating norms and procedures. Particular countries have their own political traditions and distinctive variations upon the liberal-democratic type, or, as in the case of the UK, a substantial legacy of pre-democratic norms on which the legitimacy of its political arrangements partially depends. It is precisely such differences that help explain the very different way in which the EU impacts upon the legitimacy of its individual member states, as we shall argue later in the chapter. For the present, however, it is the generic features of liberal-democratic legitimacy that are important for the next stage of our analysis.

Legitimacy and the European Union

The key question we now have to address is whether, and to what extent, these liberal-democratic criteria of legitimacy are appropriate to the institutions of the EU, and its executive, legislative and regulatory authority. A useful way of approaching this question is to examine the case for alternative models of legitimacy that have been proposed for the EU, and see what is problematic about them. One is a model of legitimacy typical of international institutions. The second is a technocratic conception of legitimacy. Both can be understood and situated within the three-fold framework already established. To assist their analysis we will present them in a pure, or ideal-typical form.

First, then, is a model of legitimacy typical of, and appropriate for, international institutions, whose membership comprises states rather than individual citizens. This is a legitimacy constructed on the one hand at the level of *legality*, by virtue of a superior jurisdiction to which national governments and legal systems are subordinate; and on the other at the level of *legitimation*, through the public recognition and affirmation by these established legitimate authorities. That is to say, the legitimacy of international institutions follows the principle: that system of authority is legitimate whose authority is recognised and confirmed by the acts of other legitimate authorities. The addressees of legitimation claims on the part of such institutions are the member states and their officials, not citizens more generally, for the simple reason that it is only the obedience and cooperation of such officials that is required for the relevant international body to achieve its purposes. From the standpoint of citizens, therefore, this model of legitimacy could be seen as an *indirect*, rather than direct, one (Wallace, 1993: 95–9; Graeger, 1994: 55–7). It is one that is wholly dependent upon the prior legitimacy of the states involved, from which international institutions in turn derive their own. This form of legitimation fits in well with the idea that political legitimacy derives essentially from the nation, and is only available to other institutions through explicit agreement of the nation's own legitimate authorities (Moravcsik, 1993).

We should note that in this model the key level of normative justifiability is rather weak, and, such as it is, depends largely on performance criteria. Like any other political body exercising jurisdiction, international institutions require justification in terms of the purposes or ends they serve, which cannot be met by other means, in this case by nation states themselves, or at the individual state level. A continuing ability to meet these purposes, therefore, would seem to be an important condition for the legitimacy of their authority. Yet such justifications rarely percolate out beyond a narrow elite group; nor do they need to, it could be argued, since these institutions are not dependent on the cooperation of a wider public to effect their purposes. It is not the direct cooperation of ordinary citizens that is required to maintain the authority of the UN, of GATT, of NATO, etc., but that of the member states and their officials; and it is for the behaviour of these alone, therefore, that considerations of legitimacy are important.

No doubt this model has been somewhat overdrawn. To say that the direct cooperation of citizens is not required by international institutions is not to say that the actions of the latter do not have significant effects on them, as anyone on the receiving end of IMF and World Bank structural adjustment policies will know. And the same goes for more benign effects. At the same time there are some areas of public policy where international institutions have now to be increasingly attentive to a global public opinion directly, as expressed by NGOs, in a way that bypasses member states themselves. Of these, human rights and environmental issues are only the most obvious. In these areas we can see a wider legitimacy, and a wider accountability, in the making. For all that, it remains true that the main source of authority for international institutions, as also the main agency for effecting their policies, is that of the member states and their officials.

How far is such a model of legitimacy applicable to the EU? There are obvious ways in which it fits quite well. Thus the authority of the EU derives primarily from its member states, through their negotiation and ratification of its successive treaties, and through their continuing participation in its decision making processes. This is legitimation by other legitimate authorities. At the same time the EU's institutions and procedures conform to the criteria of the constitutional rule of law, through a jurisdiction which is recognised as binding by the legal systems of the member states. This is the element of legality. Finally there is the important performance justification, through the increasingly evident incapacity of individual states on their own to secure the conditions for the wellbeing and security of their citizens, and the corresponding need to pool authority to complement that of the individual states. This is legitimacy through performance: the realisation of ends or purposes that cannot be met through other means.

Although this last performance justification has a resonance that reaches well beyond the narrow circle of political elites, nevertheless the form of legitimacy according to this account remains a largely *indirect* one: the legitimacy of the EU derives from that of its member states, as it is also dependent on them and their legitimacy for the implementation of its policies and the enforcement of its legislation. By the same token, if this account is correct, we could only talk of a 'legitimacy deficit' if *either* individual states had good reason for systematically questioning the EU's authority (e.g., through the European Court exceeding its jurisdiction; Weiler, 1992: 29), *or* their own legitimacy was itself eroded, so that EU policies could no longer be effectively enforced in the domestic arena.

At first sight this account of EU legitimacy according to an international institutions model looks highly plausible, and fits in well with the intergovernmental aspects of EU institutions. However, there are also a number of serious objections to it which together call into question the adequacy of a merely indirect legitimacy, mediated through that of member states, as opposed to a direct, or what Weiler calls a 'social', legitimacy (Weiler, 1992: 19–20). These objections are itemised here.

1 Whatever kind of political animal we conceive the EU to be, there is no doubt that it is the source of authoritative rules and allocations which impinge directly on citizens, and which require *their* acknowledgement of them as authoritative and binding, as well as the acknowledgement on the part of state officials (Graeger, 1994: 69–70). This is particularly true of those rules and allocations which have a potentially detrimental impact on people's livelihood, of which quota policy is only the most obvious – the preservation of fish stocks, the reduction of

agricultural surpluses, the run-down of rust-belt industries – which not only jeopardise the livelihood of individuals, but where their cooperation may be required for the effectiveness of policy (Dehousse, 1995: 3–6). It is not enough to say that enforcement is a matter for national governments, whose authority is sufficient to ensure compliance, when the source of the policy in question manifestly lies elsewhere. Moreover, the tendency of national governments to offload the odium for unpopular decisions onto the EU level only further exposes the character of its decision making and the nature of its authority to public questioning. The EU is not, after all, an impersonal force like the international market, to whose inexorable laws the impotence of governments can be safely ascribed; but a political authority like them, whose decisions are manifestly the product of responsible human agency. The more they impact directly on citizens, and require their cooperation, the more necessary becomes a direct rather than merely indirect form of legitimacy and legitimation, which acknowledges that the EU is a political system in its own right (Hix, 1994: 12–14), or at least a 'partial polity' (Wallace, 1993: 101).

2 A second objection to the adequacy of a purely indirect legitimacy concerns the significance of the supranational elements in the EU, alongside the intergovernmental ones. Although members of the Commission owe their selection to national governments, they develop a political autonomy of their own and an executive independence which escapes accountability to the governments which select them (Ludlow, 1991; Christiansen, 1996a). To be sure a similar point could be made about the international secretariats of major UN agencies, and indeed of many other international organisations. Yet there is a considerable difference between the functions of the typical international organisation, which could be seen as supplementary to those of nation states, and those of the EU, which has taken over numerous functions that were previously the preserve of its member states, and which, as noted earlier, impinge directly upon the lives of their citizens. It could of course be argued that an indirect model of legitimacy is no longer sufficient for many international organisations; but the argument is particularly strong in respect of the supranational elements in the EU, which call for forms of accountability and answerability that go beyond the mere legitimation by member governments.

3 A different objection stems from the fact that the EU is not a static institution, but a dynamic system in the process of change. Each major expansion of powers and jurisdiction raises anew the question of the authorisation and accountability of their exercise (Wallace and Smith, 1995: 148–51). It also exposes the limits of a legitimacy confined to elite agreement, with a 'permissive consensus' on the part of the rest, and its vulnerability to direct popular counter-mobilisation, as the debates over the Maastricht Treaty and monetary union have demonstrated. Whether referendums are seen as the cause of such mobilisations, or as a response to them, they constitute a powerful affirmation of the principle that the source of political authority lies directly with the people. And if it is argued that what the people are giving their democratic accolade to is a largely undemocratic set of decision making arrangements, it can equally be contended that the process of referendum itself only serves to expose the gulf between the legitimating principle required for the extension of the EU's powers, and that required for their daily exercise. If direct popular authorisation is required to legitimate an extension of powers, why not also to legitimate the agents and policies involved in their exercise?

4 The tension between the affirmation of democratic principle at one level and its denial at another is heightened by the EU's own explicit mission, which is political as well as economic and social. Its commitment to the global extension of democracy is evident in the strenuous 'democracy and human rights' hurdle which it imposes on applicants for membership, and in the less strenuous conditions it seeks in partnership arrangements with developing countries in respect of aid and other forms of support (Storey, 1995). Since the moral force of such a mission requires consistency of application, the EU can hardly avoid having the spotlight turned on its own decision procedures. Now it can of course be argued that the appropriate democratic criteria can be met *indirectly*, through the electoral authorisation of ministers at national level, and their accountability to their national parliaments. Yet the force of these procedures is relatively weak, for a number of reasons. Ministers are not explicitly authorised to fulfil a European, as opposed to a national, function. And their degree of accountability to their national parliaments is hampered by the traditions of foreign office secrecy, by the log-rolling procedures of decision making

in the Council of Ministers, and by its increasing use of majority voting (Weiler, 1992: 14). In any case, even supposing these democratic features were more robust, they would not meet the need for a direct form of legitimation, as argued in point 1.

5 A final objection to an indirect model of legitimacy for the EU lies in the impact the EU itself has on the political legitimacy of its member states. In some respects that effect can be a reinforcing one, as the EU takes responsibility for tasks that have escaped beyond the competence of individual states, for managing externalities, and so on, in a manner that may strengthen the authority of individual states (Milward, 1992: 435–47). In other respects, however, the effect is the reverse, for instance when trying to meet the Maastricht criteria for monetary union brings detrimental consequences for domestic economic policy, or when the lack of accountability in EU decision making compounds existing problems of accountability for domestic governments. The more serious these negative effects, the more they will erode the legitimacy of the member states on which the legitimacy of the EU itself depends. In other words, as we shall argue shortly, the legitimacy of political authority in the European political space is an interactive or 'two-level' process between the EU and its member states, which cannot be analysed at one level alone (Dyson, 1994: 185–92). From this perspective, a purely indirect model of legitimacy can be seen to be especially vulnerable, if the effect of EU policies is to erode the legitimacy of member states when it is the only source of its own.

Taken together, these objections constitute a powerful argument for regarding an international institutions model of indirect legitimacy as no longer sufficient for the EU, if indeed it ever was, and for the need at least to complement such a model with a more direct mode of legitimacy. Some of the objections also point strongly to the appropriateness of liberal-democratic criteria for the direct legitimation of the EU's authority. Before reaching this conclusion, however, one further model of legitimacy that has often been argued as appropriate for the EU requires consideration: the technocratic.

A technocratic version of legitimacy

A technocratic model of legitimacy is one that is very much focused on governmental performance, and on the claim that the public good is better realised through having professionals in charge, who are not subject to the vagaries, biases and distortions of democratic and especially electoral politics. Yet it is a form of legitimacy which also has a clear justification in terms of a valid source of authority, which is deemed to lie in special knowledge or expertise to which office holders have access, and which is validated by the wider legitimacy of technical, professional and scientific knowledge within modern society.

It should be said that a technocratic legitimacy is but one variant of a much more general type of legitimacy, recurrent throughout history, which claims the right to rule by virtue of access to some special knowledge, whether this be a society's traditional wisdom (traditional rule), divine revelation (theocracy), moral insight (philosopher kings), the future course of history (Marxism-Leninism), or scientific knowledge (technocracy). All of these tend to be paternalistic and anti-democratic, since they claim a privileged knowledge of what is good for society to which ordinary people have no access, whether through birth, inability, lack of opportunity or simply the division of labour. That knowledge and its authority is typically anchored in some fundamental belief system of the society, from which it derives its persuasive force.

In what ways is the technocratic version of this legitimating principle applicable to the EU? It is important to distinguish here two quite different arguments, one a purely empirical one, which shows how 'technocrats' have come in fact, through a process of depoliticisation of the decision making environment, to determine major decisions in the EU. That fact does not of itself make such an arrangement *rightful*, or give it any normative validity. Only a second explicitly normative argument, which shows that the type and character of EU decision making makes it most *appropriate* to be left to technocrats or professionals could serve to justify such a model of legitimacy.

Many writers on the EU have pointed to the strongly bureaucratic lead given to its decision making (Wallace, 1993; Wallace and Smith, 1995; Risse-Kappen, 1996, etc.). This is not only because the source of so many initiatives lies with the unelected Commission as much as with the Council of Ministers. It is also because of the fragmentation of decision making according to different policy sectors, which puts the emphasis on collaboration between separate national administrations, and the development of a common bureaucratic view about a particular area of policy.

Experts in a particular field across countries tend to share the same concerns, to speak a similar language, and to favour solutions that reflect their common values. They form what have come to be called 'epistemic communities' (Peters, 1996: 72–3) whose solutions are often simply rubber stamped by ministers (Dehousse, 1997).

Such technocratisation of decision making is not necessarily a source of legitimacy, however; indeed quite the opposite, if what is publicly expected is political control and political accountability which is more than just a facade. So a number of writers see this depoliticisation and strengthening of bureaucratic autonomy *vis à vis* national parliaments as a serious problem and a source of legitimacy deficit. Dehousse writes:

> The discrepancy between politics and policies is, of course, problematic, as many of the control mechanisms set up at national level to ensure the democratic character of policy choices ... are being eluded as a result of the integration process. There is a clear need for mechanisms to ensure the legitimacy of policy choices made in Brussels and Strasbourg. (Dehousse, 1997: 53–4)

So far, then, the mere fact of the depoliticisation of the policy environment in the EU provides no argument as to why a technocratic model should be *appropriate*. For that, explicitly normative arguments are required. These can be of two kinds. One is to say that the domination of bureaucracy within the EU is justified because it reflects a broad political consensus on the key aims of the Union – the pursuit of economic integration within a free market framework – and that decision making thereby becomes a technical matter of the implementation of agreed goals. This is a variant of the argument put by St. Simon early in the nineteenth century, to the effect that, because government in the industrial age had the aim of maximising production, it should be properly entrusted to committees of industrialists, scientists and other experts. This very sentiment has been echoed for the EU in the observation quoted by Lindberg and Scheingold that 'the major problem becomes one of maximising wealth – clearly a question for the experts, the technocrats' (Lindberg and Scheingold, 1970: 54). Weiler argues along parallel lines when he writes that the 'ideological neutrality' of the EU is a product of shelving issues of Left-Right disagreement in favour of a lowest common denominator, within a broad commitment to the free market and its extension. It is this ideological neutrality that has provided the justification for a Commission-led agenda for the EU, dominated by bureaucratic expertise; though, as Weiler also notes, this neutrality is now coming under increasing pressure (Weiler, 1992: 34–5).

A second line of argument is advanced by Majone, who takes as his starting point the claim that the main function of the EU is economic, social and legal *regulation*; and that in a modern political system such regulation is best undertaken by independent bodies – central banks, administrative tribunals, executive agencies, courts of law, regulatory bodies of all kinds – staffed by the relevant experts, whose judgements are more effective precisely because they are not subject to the sway of electoral or majoritarian pressure (Majone, 1997). In fact Majone defends the technocratic principle both on the broad political grounds that it enables many of the deep cleavages in the EU to be successfully managed, as well as for its qualities of regulatory judgement – consistency, fairness, independence, and so forth. He draws a distinction between two conceptions of democracy, which he calls majoritarian and non-majoritarian: the one which subjects all decisions to majority control, and the other which 'attempts to restrain majority rule by placing public authority in the hands of officials who have limited or no direct accountability to either political majority or minorities' (Majone, 1997: 286). The former type of democracy, he argues, is appropriate where politics is essentially about questions of distribution and redistribution; the latter where its task is primarily that of regulation, as in the EU. He draws on US experience to show how such regulatory bodies could meet democratic criteria of fairness, transparency, public accountability, etc., in the absence of any direct electoral answerability; indeed better, precisely because of the absence of the latter.

How far are these normative arguments for technocratic legitimacy in the EU valid? They raise some fundamental questions about the nature of politics which go back as far as Plato, if not beyond, as well as more particular issues relevant to EU decision making. Most basic is the epistemological question addressed in Plato's dialogues, about how far 'the good' for society can be certainly known (Plato, 1961; 1976). Are the ends of public life knowable, and, if so, by whom? Are they a matter of technical or professional expertise, so that they should be entrusted to the relevant experts or technicians, as you would your car servicing? Or are they a matter of choice of priority between competing goods, or competing conceptions of the good life, of the kind which ordinary people make, and are capable of making, in their own personal lives? If the latter, then of course technical and professional expertise will be required to help clarify possible policy choices, and the relative feasibility and costs of different options, but not to determine the choices themselves, which are irreducibly *evaluative*.

It is a basic assumption of both liberal and democratic thought that politics conforms to the latter rather than the former model: that it involves a matter of value choice between competing priorities, whose test is its acceptability to a relevant public or publics, not a matter of definitive solution by experts. In the specific context of debates about the EU, the fact that policy making may have become 'depoliticised' in terms of a loss of democratic accountability does not mean that it has thereby also become depoliticised in the sense of becoming free from value choice, and thereby a purely technical matter. Even broad definitions of goals, such as the maximisation of wealth or economic integration, conceal a myriad of value choices in terms of their implementation, which can never be reduced to the merely technical (Beetham, 1996: 31–2). And regulatory frameworks always have implicit if not explicit policy choices built into them, which carry distributional consequences, such as a central bank's priority in the control of inflation (Caporaso, 1996: 43–4). If so, who is to determine which these essentially political choices are to be? The fact that some of the 'ideological neutrality' supposedly built into the EU is now itself coming under challenge, as in demands for a more employment-oriented policy, and in basic disagreements about how this might be achieved, suggests that this neutrality belongs to a particular historical phase, not to the essence of EU decision making as such.

Majone's argument merits a more specific rebuttal. It is based upon a comparison with US regulatory agencies, and what he terms their 'procedural as well as substantive' legitimacy. Procedural legitimacy implies that:

> the agencies are created by democratically enacted statutes which define the agencies' legal authority and objectives; that the regulators are appointed by elected officials; that regulatory decision-making follows formal rules, which often require public participation; that agency decisions must be justified and are open to judicial review.
>
> (Majone, 1997: 291)

What Majone fails to acknowledge is that the distinctively *democratic* features of this procedural legitimacy in the US are completely lacking in the EU; yet these are precisely needed if this regulatory legitimacy is to have any democratic credentials at all. Indeed his contrast between majoritarian and non-majoritarian forms of democracy obscures the fact that electoral democracy and electoral legitimation comprise a necessary complement to the criteria of fairness, transparency and accountability, if regulatory agencies are to secure the wider legitimacy they need for the essentially political dimension of their role. Few would doubt the need for a measure of independence in regulatory bodies, but they also require a wider democratic framework in which their broad objectives are to be set.

This brings us to two further, more democracy-friendly, versions of the technocratic argument. One is the argument that, by taking certain issues out of electoral control and depoliticising them, the quality of democracy can thereby actually be *enhanced*. This can either happen because, by putting some aspects of, for example, economic policy, such as interest rates or exchange rate policy, in the hands of 'experts', political control over the rest can be made more effective. What is lost in breadth of control is more than made up for by depth, so the argument runs. This example of course depends on contestable assumptions about economic relationships, or at least about economic priorities. Another way is exemplified by the idea of a bill of rights, which seeks to make certain democratic rights more secure (the freedoms of speech, assembly, association, etc.) precisely by putting them beyond the reach of political or majoritarian erosion, and making them subject to defence and adjudication by independent courts. It is only in countries where parliamentary sovereignty has been elevated into the supreme democratic principle that this move could be seen as a surrender, rather than an essential guarantor, of democracy.

This form of the 'technocratic' argument, however, acknowledges the primacy of democratic legitimacy, to which it sees technocratic judgement as a complement, rather than as a competitor or replacement. In other words, the latter's justification is to be found in the contribution it makes to more effective democratic control over policy, not independently in some self-sufficient technocratic authority. So this argument does not really count as a form of technocratic legitimacy at all.

21

Much the same could be said about a second argument, to the effect that a technocratic form of government could be legitimated as a temporary or transitional necessity, until the conditions for democratisation had been sufficiently developed (see Wallace and Smith, 1995: 144). This argument would parallel an argument about the preconditions for democratisation at the state level: viz., that effective structures of political decision making with authority across the given territory, and mutual confidence between political elites, have to be established before the system is exposed to the pressures of popular involvement and electoral competition. Democracy has to be postponed, in other words, in order that it may be made possible at all (Hall, 1993).

Whatever one thinks about this argument, it should be evident that it does not make technocracy an independent alternative to a democratic legitimacy, on which it remains parasitic, and to which it is therefore vulnerable once serious demands for popular authorisation and accountability are raised. Even as a temporary expedient, however, technocratic forms of rule suffer from the characteristic delusion that the decision-makers 'know best', that their decisions are merely technical or instrumental, and that they can be assumed to be benevolent agents of the public good. So this version can no more than the previous one be regarded as a serious alternative to democratic legitimacy.

Legitimacy deficits in the European Union

Our argument so far, then, is that an indirect conception of legitimacy, based on the model of international institutions, which derives from legality on the one hand and recognition by other legitimate authorities on the other, is insufficient on its own to provide legitimacy for the institutions and decisional authority of the EU. At the same time a purely technocratic model of direct legitimacy is inadequate to the political character of its decision making. Only a direct form of legitimacy which is based upon the liberal democratic criteria of normative validity and legitimation will be able to ensure citizen support and loyalty to its authority. These are the criteria of effective performance in respect of agreed ends, democratic authorisation, accountability and representation, and agreement on the identity and boundaries of the political community, respectively. Performance, democracy, identity: these

22

three liberal-democratic criteria of legitimacy are relevant to the authority of the EU, as they are to that of its member states.

Naturally it does not follow that the only way in which these criteria can be fulfilled is through the institutional forms typical of the nation state. Nor does it mean that the liberal-democratic criteria have to replace, rather than be complemented by, the indirect criteria appropriate to international institutions. Indeed, for the foreseeable future the legitimacy of the EU will need to operate according to both modes, the direct and the indirect, the supranational and the intergovernmental together (Dehousse, 1995: 22–6). And one of its recurrent problems is how to reconcile the tensions between these two modes of legitimation. This will be discussed in more detail later.

Our conclusion for the moment, then, is that a significant element of direct legitimacy conforming to liberal-democratic criteria is now necessary for the EU. To say that it is necessary, however, is not to say that it is yet sufficiently realised, or even that it can be. Here the idea of a 'legitimacy deficit' becomes appropriate. It should be clear, however, that such a concept only makes sense if one has first established the *necessity* for a given level or type of legitimacy, and much of the literature on legitimacy deficit in the EU fails to do this, or simply assumes it without argument. Much of it also assumes that the only dimension of deficit that matters is the democratic one, when, as we shall show (and as others have also suggested, Weiler, 1992; Graeger, 1994; Christiansen, 1996b), it occurs in all three spheres of performance, democracy and identity together. Indeed, it is the complex interaction between the three, and the way in which solving a deficit in one sphere creates or intensifies problems in another, that provides one of the keys to understanding the subject of legitimacy in the EU. We will take each in turn.

Performance

There are two possible sources of legitimacy deficit here. One is the existence of fundamental disagreement about the character and scope of the tasks the EU should undertake: the definition of the ends or purposes it should serve. A second concerns the ability of its institutional matrix to deliver effective policy in the areas it undertakes, to meet sòme basic criteria of effective decision making, and to demonstrate a capacity for correction and renewal in the event of 'failure'. Basic ideological disagreement and institutional ineffectiveness are the two forms of legitimacy deficit in the sphere of 'performance'.

As to the first of these, we might usefully distinguish two different kinds of fundamental ideological disagreement about the character and scope of the EU's tasks. One has a primarily nationalist focus, and takes place between those who see certain governmental functions as irreducibly national, and their surrender to the European level as a betrayal of the state's responsibility, on the one side, and those who take a much more pragmatic view of where governmental functions should be located, on the other. This dispute is complicated by the fact that what are seen as the irreducible functions of the nation state may vary from country to country, and may include control of the currency, internal affairs, immigration policy, as well as security and defence policy and foreign affairs more widely. Whatever the precise content, defining certain issues as an irreducibly national responsibility makes their treatment at the European level by definition illegitimate.

Overlapping and cutting across the above divide is a Right-Left disagreement about whether, or how far, the EU is a free-market or a 'social' Europe, a bankers' or a people's Europe, a Europe of social exclusion or of full employment. Although this disagreement forms part of the normal stuff of politics at the national level, and its replication at the European level could be seen as an important step towards the 'normalisation' of politics within the EU, nevertheless it also becomes a reason for disputing the legitimacy of the EU's decision making itself.

Both these ideological divisions about the scope and character of the EU's tasks are complicated by the integrationist dynamic of its development, and by considerations of the EU as a process, not just an established set of institutions. According to a certain neo-functionalist logic, it can be argued that the different policy areas are inter-related, and that one set of functions can only be effectively fulfilled if the scope of policy is extended into adjacent areas, as, for example, the free market requires a 'level playing field' in social costs and provision, or the establishment of a common currency. A more political version of this argument holds that the credibility of the EU depends on its maintaining a certain dynamic to the extension of its functions; that it cannot afford to stand still for more than relatively short periods of consolidation, but must continually renew its political momentum if it is to sustain its place in the public consciousness in the face of the much more powerful publicity resources available to its member states. Both versions have been evident in debates over the single currency.

If we accept any validity to this argument, in either version, then we are confronted with significant legitimacy dilemmas. On the one hand, the necessity or at least the desirability of moving into new policy areas in order to meet established goals more effectively exposes the EU to an intensification of ideological disagreement about its proper scope and purpose. At the same time, taking more policy areas out of the hands of national parliaments accentuates the EU's democratic deficit in respect of popular authorisation and accountability. Although the first of these dilemmas could in principle be resolved by subjecting all major new extensions of function to national referenda, and using the popular will to 'trump' other definitions of the national interest, such a device, as already argued, will not of itself remove the democratic inadequacy of its ongoing decisional processes.

A second feature of potential performance deficit in the EU relates to the effectiveness of its decision-making procedures. As will be evident from our argument so far, we regard effectiveness in the attainment of the agreed ends or purposes of government as an important component of legitimacy, rather than as something separate from it, as some other writers do (Lipset, 1958; Ludlow, 1991). Of course what counts as 'effective' is a matter of some dispute. Yet the distinctive difficulties of reaching agreement at all in an intergovernmental institution such as the Council of Ministers, when faced with the ongoing complexity of its problems, has led to a number of procedural solutions which have in turn intensified the democratic dimension of the legitimacy deficit. One is the process of 'log-rolling', whereby compromises on one issue are traded off against another issue in a complex package which defies any systematic transparency or accountability. Another is the progressive introduction of majority voting, which makes it difficult to hold ministers individually accountable for decisions which they may well have been outvoted on (Edwards, 1996). Both are typical examples of the way in which solving problems in one domain exacerbates legitimacy problems in another, in this case the democratic deficit, to which we now turn.

Democracy

The so-called 'democratic deficit' is one of the most frequently discussed features of legitimacy in the EU. It is usually identified as a lack of popular consent (Weiler, 1992; Wallace and Smith, 1995). Yet, as our analysis so far has suggested, 'consent' is an unhelpful concept in analysing liberal-democratic legitimacy. This is because, first, we need to draw a clear distinction between the procedure (typically a referendum) whereby popular agreement is explicitly sought for a major extension of the EU's jurisdiction, and the ongoing legitimacy of its decision making authority. But then, secondly, the latter is much better analysed through the democratic criteria of authorisation, accountability and representation, than through the much vaguer concept of 'consent', which can include anything from states of mind to acts of explicit authorisation or agreement.

If we take each of these three in turn – authorisation, accountability, representation – then the authority of the EU's institutions can be readily shown to be deficient in each of these aspects of a direct democratic legitimacy. In respect of *authorisation*, neither the members of the Commission nor the Council of Ministers are popularly authorised. Commission members are appointed by national governments, while the Council Ministers, although they may be popularly elected, are elected by national electorates to fulfil an explicitly national, not a European, function. How this evident deficit might be met is open to some dispute. As a minimum, it would require the election of the President of the Commission, either directly or through the European Parliament, to act as a counter-weight to the indirectly elected Council of Ministers (Bogdanor, 1986; Ludlow, 1991; Williams, 1991). The Commission is the manifestly supranational element in EU institutions. It possesses the power of initiative in legislative and policy matters. Having its President popularly elected, preferably directly, would not only in itself substantially enhance the democratic legitimacy of the EU, by deriving its presidential authority directly from the people. It would also accelerate a democratic trend which is already embryonic: the practice of the Commission addressing key publics directly, rather than only through governments, and having to exercise political persuasion to win support for their measures, which is the essence of democratic politics, and a key factor in enhancing the acceptability of policy.

A recurrent problem in all proposals for reducing the democratic deficit is how to reconcile a direct democratic legitimacy with the requirements of an indirect or intergovernmental legitimacy: in this case, how to reconcile the direct popular authorisation of the Commission President with the selection of its members by individual governments. Here the problem is perhaps least acute, since presumably the Commission members could continue to be proposed by governments, to ensure a national balance, while particular portfolios could also continue to be at the disposal of the President, to whom the other members would be ultimately accountable, albeit under the doctrine of collective or cabinet responsibility. The problem of reconciling the two modes of legitimacy becomes much more acute when we move into the area of wider democratic accountability, which is commonly agreed to be one of the most serious deficiencies of EU decision making.

With regard to democratic *accountability*, as we have seen, the individual accountability of Council Ministers to their domestic parliaments is tenuous at best. On the other hand, the collective accountability of either the Commission or the Council directly to the European Parliament is limited by the restrictions on the latter's powers of scrutiny, amendment and approval of legislation and expenditure. Enhancing these powers would be an obvious way to reduce this deficit. Yet it would also conflict with some of the current conditions for intergovernmental agreement in the Council of Ministers. Carefully packaged agreements negotiated across a range of issues simultaneously could easily become unravelled if they were subject to separate amendment by the Parliament, or even if they became a matter of public knowledge, as any effective democratic accountability would require (Lodge, 1994). The dilemma here is whether the two modes of legitimacy, direct and indirect, are not mutually contradictory rather than complementary (Graeger, 1994: 52–5; Christiansen, 1996b: 5–6).

Extending the powers of the Parliament to ensure more effective accountability would also raise acutely the question of democratic *representation*. There are a number of different issues here. One is that elections to the European Parliament currently have the character of 'second-order' elections, in which the turnout is low, and the outcomes are determined by the respective national standing of the competing parties, and by national agendas, rather than European ones. Although a Parliament with greater powers might generate more interest, because more would hang on the result, this is by no means certain. Would the level of popular legitimacy of, say, a typical UK local authority be sufficient to sustain a more empowered and active EP? A second problem concerns which form of representation is most appropriate, given that the respective national electoral systems all differ so widely. The consolidation of democratic legitimacy through popular representation is only effective to the extent that the form of representation itself meets with broad agreement.

At this point protagonists of a 'consociational' form of democracy would argue that the consociational model is the most appropriate for the EU, since it locates the basis of popular representation in the nation and national electorates, and requires the political elites so elected to reach a negotiated consensus on policy and legislation, rather than taking decisions by simple majority (see Weiler *et al.*, 1995: 28–33). This view of course privileges the Council of Ministers over the Parliament as the key democratic forum in the EU. In practice the consociational model is simply another form of intergovernmentalism in disguise, and fails to recognise either that many of the major divisions on European issues no longer run along national lines, or the reasons already advanced as to why a direct form of democratic legitimacy is now necessary to sustain the authority of the EU's institutions and legislation.

The main dilemma raised by the extension of democratic legitimacy through more effective authorisation, accountability and representation in fact lies elsewhere: in the question of whether there exists sufficient sense of common identity among the peoples of Europe for elections to bear the weight expected of them. The divisiveness of competitive electoral politics, it could be argued, is only sustainable on the basis of a more fundamental unity such as agreement on political nationhood typically provides at the level of member states. Once issues of political identity are themselves brought into play in electoral politics, and become a major source of electoral division, then democracy becomes unsustainable, since electoral minorities lack the necessary trust in the majority that their vital interests will be protected. On this view, any further democratisation of the EU cannot run too far ahead of the development of a more robust sense of common identity among the European electorate, and a fuller acceptance of the appropriateness of a European level of governance (Weiler, 1992: 22). This is necessary even if such democratisation remains complemented by the intergovernmental institutions that are rooted in more distinctive national loyalties. In this necessity lies the basis for a third dimension of legitimacy deficit.

Identity

Most commentators are agreed that a sense of European identity and loyalty is embryonic at best among the European electorate. There is considerable disagreement, however, about how such a loyalty might be developed. To be sure, existing national identities are partly constructed identities, through processes of myth making and 'inventions of tradition', as well as through conscious administrative and cultural policy. Yet the European level lacks some of those longstanding elements which typically form the sediment of nationhood, whether a common language, shared customs, or a common historical experience, on the basis of which the consciousness of a distinctive and valued identity can be shaped and given political significance (Smith, 1992). Europeans possess no common language; the only longstanding shared culture is a high, not a popular, culture; and the shared history of twentieth century wars can still be as much a source of national antagonism as of a common determination to avoid their recurrence. These elements seem rather tenuous when compared with the mobilising power of the nation state, and its virtual monopoly, even now, of the public media of communication and of cultural and educational policy.

Such considerations are only conclusive, however, if we think of political identities and loyalties in ethnic, or backward referring terms, based upon a common past, rather than upon an agreed political project for a common future (Habermas, 1992; Wagner, 1993). If we think in the latter terms, there is some ground for optimism about the development of a European identity, based upon the construction of a common European citizenship and agreement on a shared political future (Meehan, 1993; Welsh, 1993). Central here would be the guarantee of key rights to all European citizens across the European political space, wherever they happen to live and work: civil and political rights, basic economic, social and cultural rights, equality of respect and opportunity regardless of social or national differences, etc. The guarantee of these rights as the central public feature of the Union would give everyone confidence that their basic interests would not be infringed by any electoral defeat, and would serve to limit what was at stake in the electoral contest.

29

In any case we are not talking about the outright replacement of national loyalties by a European one, so much as reducing the *exclusivity* of political loyalties at the level of the nation state, and moving towards a more pluralistic conception in which the European, the national, the regional and the local might coexist (Laffan, 1996: 98–9). And while the European loyalty was still embryonic, there would be an argument for limiting the development of direct democratic forms in the EU, and for the continuation of the inter-governmental component, for all the difficulty this in turn poses at the levels of effective performance and democratic accountability.

In conclusion, this account of the different aspects of legitimacy deficit in the EU suggests that what we are confronted with is not only different legitimacy deficits, but also a set of what might be termed legitimacy *dilemmas*, whereby the strategies for resolving a legitimacy deficit in one sphere – whether of performance, democracy or identity – result in displacing the deficit onto another sphere, rather than resolving it outright. This is because of the inherent interconnectedness of the different spheres. We should thus perhaps think in terms of the management of dilemmas rather than the solution of deficits. And how well or badly they are managed lies partly in the hands of the policy-makers, and particularly in the hands of the Commission itself. After all, as Barker notes, the reproduction and consolidation of political legitimacy is not something just given, but also depends upon the actions (and inactions) of state personnel themselves (Barker, 1990: 138–194).

Legitimacy at the EU and state levels

We have argued, then, that the legitimacy of the EU can only be understood in terms of the relation between the different spheres or components of legitimacy – performance, democracy and identity, respectively. There is a further set of interconnections to be considered, however, and that is between the European and the national levels. This is because the manner in which legitimacy deficits and dilemmas are managed at the EU level will have consequences for the political legitimacy of member states, and for the balance of political forces within them. In addition, such consequences can be expected to impact *differentially* rather than uniformly on the different member states, insofar as the distinctive characteristics of their national identity, domestic democracy and state performance prove more or less compatible with the developmental requirements of the EU. Some of these differences will be merely outlined here, and will be given fuller treatment in the rest of the book.

At the level of governmental performance, it is a plausible hypothesis that the opportunities provided by the EU level are more likely to enhance the capacities of small states, and regions within states, than of large ones; and that, as between states of a similar size, the EU will enjoy greater support to the extent that it is seen to offer higher levels of, say, economic and social rights protection, or administrative competence, than the corresponding domestic jurisdiction, and vice versa. This would explain the strong support for the EU in Belgium, Ireland, Luxembourg and The Netherlands, compared with Scandinavia. Among larger states, the history of Italy's government gives it better reason than most to view governance by the EU favourably. It is difficult to imagine elsewhere the acceptance of a special EU tax to meet the Maastricht convergence criteria; in contrast, meeting these criteria has plunged the domestic polities of France and Germany into crisis.

At the democratic level, membership of the EU can be expected to help consolidate the legitimacy of states which have relatively recently democratised (in southern and eastern Europe), through the high threshold set and monitored by the associated institutions of the Council of Europe, as well as the less tangible 'neighbourhood' effects of EU membership itself. On the other hand, for a state such as the UK, where democracy is intimately linked to the sovereignty of the Westminster Parliament, the development of direct democratic authorisation and representation at the EU level is bound to present more of a challenge to domestic political legitimacy than for those states whose constitution validates a spatial separation of powers between centre and regions, and their respective electorates. Such states are also likely to be able to accommodate the idea of multiple political identities more readily.

Similarly, when it comes to questions of national identity, some are more readily compatible with a sense of being European than others (Laffan, 1996: 86). The reconstruction of a German, or more precisely West German, national identity since 1945 hinged on constructing that identity as also European, so that it could no longer present a threat to its neighbouring states. The UK, by contrast, with its strong Atlantic and Commonwealth connections, has always presented itself as a reluctant European, and has had great difficulty since 1945 in defining a positive image for itself that is not backward-looking and isolationist, and one that is therefore threatened by the idea of a European citizenship. Most of the other member states of the Union occupy positions between these two poles, though sentiment is obviously not uniform within them, whether between regions, classes or generations.

These examples, sketchy though they are, should suffice to show that political legitimacy in Europe cannot be analysed at one level alone, whether that of the EU or its component states, but is a 'two-level' matter of the interrelationship between both levels, and of the differential impact of the EU on the legitimacy of its different member states. Identifying and explaining some of these differences will be an important task for the remainder of this volume.

Conclusion

It will be helpful to summarise the main conclusions of our analysis so far in propositional form:

1 EU institutions increasingly require a degree of direct or substantive legitimacy alongside the procedural legitimacy derived from the respective treaties, and the indirect legitimation provided by member states.

2 Such legitimacy can only be found in the three criteria of normative validity characteristic of liberal-democratic polities, though the institutional forms through which they are realised may differ, and are still in the process of evolution.

3 Resolving legitimacy deficits in any one sphere (of performance, democracy or identity) may simply displace the problem to another one, or conflict with the requirements of an indirect legitimation; so that managing legitimacy 'dilemmas' may well be the main issue to be addressed.

4 In respect of all three criteria, political legitimacy in Europe involves an interactive process between the EU and national levels, which cannot be analysed exclusively at either one.

5 The EU impacts differentially on the legitimacy of its member states, according to their respective size, character and distinctive legitimation problems.

These propositions will provide the basis for our more detailed analysis in the chapters that follow.

CHAPTER TWO

Identity

Introduction

The absence of a shared collective identity is often considered the most serious of the obstacles to the development of political legitimacy at the European level. There are two ways in which people might claim that governance is not 'rightful': one is to say that decisions are taken in the right political unit but by an illegitimate procedure; the other is to say that decisions have been taken by an acceptable procedure but in a collectivity that has no right to expect their cooperation. Where people do not feel a part of the unit in question, its acts may be experienced as an outrageous interference, rather than as a pleasing exercise in self-governance by a well-defined community. In the case of liberal democratic value systems, the link between the legitimacy of the unit and that of the political process is a peculiarly intimate one. Not only does the principle of popular sovereignty presuppose that the question of who constitutes the people has been settled to mutual agreement (Rousseau, 1963: 173; Dahl, 1989); the procedures of democratic decision making, especially that of majority decision, require sufficient trust between citizens for them to accept that being outvoted does not constitute a threat to their identity or essential interests. At the level of the state, it is nationhood that has historically been seen as providing the necessary sense of common identity and mutual trust for democracy to work. Can there be an equivalent at the European level?

Against this background, it is unsurprising that attempts to theorise the relationship between identity, legitimacy and the EU's institutional development have marked important milestones in the intellectual history of European integration. Even what we might now consider to be a minimalist definition of integration – 'dependable expectations' that political change would only occur by peaceable means – was thought by Karl Deutsch to require a 'sense of community', 'mutual sympathies' and a 'we-feeling' (Deutsch *et al.*, 1957: 36). But, when it came to the tougher challenge of integrating separate European states into a single political system, the early post-war federalist movement foundered on the objection that such an institutional order could not be willed into existence in a single federating moment. For, without a sense of shared political identity, a Euro-government would, it was felt, be ignored, lack authority, under perform and eventually fall into ridicule (Harrison, 1974). The baton thus passed to those who were prepared to consider how European identity, legitimacy and institutions might develop incrementally and interactively. The so-called neofunctionalists sought to show how integration could cumulate from one policy area to another, and how transnational political identities could, correspondingly, spill over from one elite to another before embracing a wider public. In a phrase that is often quoted, Ernst Haas defined integration as a process in which organised 'political actors' would be gradually persuaded to shift their 'loyalties and expectations' towards a new centre (Haas, 1958: 12–13). Later reflections in the same genre presented elites as diffusing the new identity across classes and social groups through the pluralistic political activities of parties and interest groups (Schmitter, 1971).

In contrast, intergovernmentalists have insisted on the need to rethink European integration from the assumption that political identities would, and should, remain national in character. President De Gaulle feared that supranational constructions would produce a legitimacy vacuum. States that were of diminishing importance to their physical and economic well-bring would lose public loyalty without this being picked up by supranational institutions that lacked any basis in public sentiment. Europe would, as a result, be all the more easily dominated from the outside (Kolodziej, 1974). Amongst academic intergovernmentalists, Stanley Hoffman has argued that patterns of international co-operation would adapt to obstinately national patterns of identity, rather than the other way round (Hoffman, 1966; Tranholm-Mikkelsen, 1991: 8). More recently, Andrew Moravcsik has constructed one of the most influential theories of the 1990s from the assumption that preferences on major issues of European integration would continue to be formed in the domestic arena. Because they are the only institutions that correspond to relatively uncontested identities, only national democracies have, in Moravcsik's view, the capacity to settle major arguments authoritatively. Major measures of integration have, accordingly, to be theorised as a two-stage bargaining process in which Union negotiations begin from – and are always constrained by – the interests of legitimately formed majorities in the major member states. (Moravcsik, 1991; 1993). So, in sum, an important distinction between the contending schools of thought that dominate the study of European integration – supranational/neofunctionalist and intergovernmentalist – is to be found in the different assumptions they make the possibility and validity of European identity formation. But to the extent that even neofunctionalists anticipate that European identity would be tenuous at the beginning of the integration process – and that the Union would, accordingly, need to piggy-back for a time on the legitimating force of the state (Wallace and Smith, 1995: 139) – there is an overlap between the two schools. Both seem to agree that of our three dimensions of legitimacy – identity, democracy and performance – the first is likely to be the weakest link for the EU.

Pathways to European identity formation

Now, there are those who argue that there is a shared sense of European political identity on which the Union can begin to draw. To be European, according to this view, is to live in a society which has developed through a distinctive series of historical stages. The cumulative legacy of classical thought, Christianity, the Renaissance and the Enlightenment, industrialisation and modernisation (Davies, 1996: 1278) has, it is suggested, endowed those who live in the EU with broadly compatible views on the appropriate ends and methods of legitimate government: liberal democracy, pluralism and commitment to the 'open society', rule of law, equality of civic–legal entitlements and a measure of public responsibility for social welfare are all values that are to be found in substantial measure in all Union countries. As Paul Howe has put it, mainstream political forces in Western Europe tend to be commensurable, even where they are diverse and competitive (Howe, 1997: 313). Long suppressed by nation state monopolies on mass identity formation these commonalities may, conversely, begin to ground

35

a political identity now that there are Union institutions to nurture them.

In addition, optimists argue, the Union has both a foundation myth and a telos. The idea that the Community was founded to avoid a repetition of the 'European civil wars' of 1914–8 and 1939–45 is an emotionally compelling justification for integration, as well as a standing criticism of the ancien regime in which the alternative to unification is presented as an undisciplined states system liable to consume its own children. Meanwhile the goal of 'ever closer Union' provides the EU with a forward looking identity and a common enterprise. Even for the less starry eyed, this may be cashed out in a more prosaic sense that Europeans are all in the same boat: that they form a 'community of fate' in the face of globalisation and other concentrations of power in international system.

If some claim that all of this is identity enough to begin to ground the legitimacy of a supranational political system, others are more sceptical. They argue that the historical experiences of those who live in the EU are as likely to divide as unite, and the same is true of attempts to formulate visions of European integration. Nor is the Union yet territorially bounded or stabilised. With no clear end to the process of widening, the EU's citizens do not know precisely who they will have to bond with to form a new political solidarity. The staggered character of likely enlargements to the East also means that the Union will, for a long time to come, contain national publics that are at very different stages of political socialisation into its institutional system. It may also come under pressure to admit countries whose own identities are problematic, exclusivist or otherwise likely to compromise those forms of identity that are workable at the European level. Above all, it is objected, the EU has no prospect of rivalling the nation as a form of identity, and, those who believe it has, woefully misunderstand the distinctive character of nationhood. For even if it is true that loyalties have always been complex in Europe, the nation has been the carrier of a special authority to contain and arbitrate those more diffuse identities in a manner that made democracy and ordered government possible (Smith, 1991). It is this special legitimacy that may now be non-transferable to the European level. One version of this argument emphasises the Union's lack of ethnocultural homogeneity. According to one recent article, it lacks a 'mythical foundation' and an 'ethnic affiliation' without which it is difficult to 'stabilise and institutionalise' its community (Obradovic, 1996: 209, 215).

An alternative form of scepticism about the possibility of a European political solidarity rejects foregoing suggestions that identities need be ethnically primordial and accepts that they may, instead, be constructed; but it goes on to suggest that the nation state may have been put together as a kind of 'final equilibrium' in identity formation and that this limits the transferability of political loyalties to the EU (Cederman, 1996: 4). Because nations aligned a whole series of factors – uniform civic–legal entitlements, an economic division of labour, welfare responsibilities, stabilised political boundaries and such ethnic homogeneity as could be called into existence – in a single body politic they quite literally assumed an 'organic character' (Smith, 1991: 69). With the passing of time, several generations were born into the nation. Its more created characteristics receded into the past and it acquired the largely uncontested political authority of a 'natural community'. The difficulties this presents to the EU are twofold. First, the factors that produced national identities are non-repeatable either at EU level or in contemporary circumstances: governance and cultural 'life worlds' can no longer be easily aligned with well defined political boundaries, and political authorities no longer have the resources to make the man-made appear natural. Second, it is suggested, the nation state is a 'frozen political identity' capable of dominating public sentiments and loyalties well after the decline of the conditions that gave rise to it. It continues to control key institutions by which collective identities are reproduced, notably the education system. Others, such as language, political debate and news media, have tended to stabilise around the nation state and to give it self-reinforcing cognitive frontiers in the political domain, even where its boundaries are physically porous or much penetrated by other, less political, cultural flows. The nation, therefore, remains the dominant arena for political socialisation. No other political system is as well understood or as readily transmitted between generational cohorts (Zetterholm, 1994). When attempts have been made to create a European political arena, notably with direct elections to the European Parliament, it is the Euro-politicians who have had to adapt to compartmentalised national debates and identities, rather than the other way round. All of this leaves the Union conspicuously vulnerable to nationalistic counter-mobilisations or to disintegration in moments of stress.

So, to summarise, the last two arguments indicate that the Union will tend to be 'captured' by its pre-existing national identities and thus constrained from developing an identity of its own. Before examining whether there are any plausible escape routes from this predicament, we need, however, to note that the type of identity needed for a legitimate and viable Union will, in part, be linked to the kind of political system it purports to be. The possibility that it might function as a non-state political system would substantially lessen the challenge of identity formation (Schmitter, 1995: 349–50; Weiler, 1997a: 260). For, if the Union has no need to command a monopoly of violence, to spill the blood of its population, to dig deep into the taxpayer's pocket, or to be the final rule-making body in all areas of policy, it will obviously make far lighter demands on the loyalties and cooperation of its citizens than the nation state.

On the other hand, it will be hard to remove the need for some kind of EU political identity altogether. The Union may need to make substantial allocations of political values if it is to meet the performance requirements of legitimacy (see Chapter 4). It will often need to override nation states with all their historically accumulated authority. The more such a Euroconstitutionalism – 'behaviour as if the founding instrument were not a treaty governed by international law but a constitutional charter governed by constitution law' (Weiler, 1997a: 97) – comes to shape the rules that govern economy and society, the more the public may learn to differentiate between actions that originate at the two levels of government, so making it more difficult to secure citizen cooperation by disguising Union policies as national policies mediated through domestic institutions. Some may also begin to argue that the Union cannot pretend to draw its legitimacy from the very units that it so frequently overrides.

Such problems may require the Union to seek a more direct form of democratic legitimation and it is this requirement which will, in many ways, shape the kind of political identity that it will have to develop. We hypothesise that it will need to be capable of the following: first, of making people feel that voting in Euro-elections is a citizen obligation – for, as rational choice theorists remind us, participation is likely to be low where voting is considered to be no more than a cost-benefit calculation (Downs, 1957); second, of encouraging people to vote in such contests with European and not national priorities in mind; third, of supporting a

European public forum of shared communications and debate; and, fourth, of producing widespread public acceptance of trans-nationally defined democratic outcomes, though consideration of whether these need be majoritarian in character we hold over until the next chapter. With these demands on European identity formation in mind, we now look at different ways in which it might occur. These are intended to be cumulative, rather than self-contained, suggestions. In other words, of the three different pathways to European identity formation that we are about to review, both of the last two notions fills some gap or deficiency in the idea which preceded it.

I. A second look at the constructivist route

There are plenty of examples of the EU using its political resources to cultivate a sense of identity. These include direct elections to the European Parliament in which some 60 per cent of citizens have participated every five years since 1979; use of the European Courts as a means of appeal against national authorities; attempts to develop a concept of EU citizenship; adoption of a flag and anthem; the Socrates network of student exchanges; the introduction of a Union passport; and, of course, the single currency. Some of these measures have classic characteristics of purposeful identity formation: the use of symbolism (the flag); the construction of insider-outsider relationships (passports and citizen rights); occasional acts of citizen mobilisation and participation (voting); and use of everyday objects to create permanent reminders of the presence and authority of the political system (single currency). If most political communities are imagined into existence (Anderson, 1991), and if the nation was created to meet the functional needs of modernity (Gellner, 1983: 110), what is to stop a European identity being willed into being in response to the transnationalisation of many public needs? As Fritz Scharpf. has put it,

> above the level of primary groups, collective identities are socially constructed from often quite heterogeneous constituents . . . just as playing together can create teams, living under a common government, and participating in common political processes, can create political identities. For that reason the institutional structure of the Union is by no means irrelevant for the future evolution of the Union. (Sharpf, 1997: 20)

Many political systems have been pieced together from multicultural communities. The question is not whether such an approach is possible, but of how to create the right mix between institutional order, social compromise and political culture as to ground a successful identity, rather than a dysfunctional one. The challenge is one of creating a United States or a Switzerland, rather than a Canada or a Belgium (Scharpf, 1997: 20).

Now, we have already encountered the most obvious obstacle placed across the constructivist pathway to European integration: the pre-emption of the politics of mass identity by the nation state, the unwillingness of domestic elites to allow another 'political centre' to 'service' cultural reproduction for fear that it might not do this with 'impartiality' (Gellner, 1983: 119; Cederman, 1996: 12), and the ease with which states can keep a hold on the Union by 'an intensive incorporation of national actors into the whole EC process' (Wessels, 1997: 281). But is such a constraint on the formation of an autonomous European identity unshiftable? One reason to feel that it may not be is that there are profound difficulties with the idea of states creating a European Union and, then, keeping it all to themselves. The hypothesis that governments can displace the satisfaction of key needs into the Union, while retaining a monopoly of identity at national level, simply will not do. The Europeanisation of policies is usually led by elected politicians anxious to avoid a squeeze between public expectations and diminishing state capacity. Results need to be delivered within the limited time frames of the electoral cycle (Marks et al., 1996: 348) and under conditions of considerable uncertainty. This puts governments under pressure to admit sub-national actors to the European arena, to organise those with knowledge and resources relevant to successful policy performance into stable policy communities at EU level (Peterson, 1995; Richardson, 1996: 14) and to proselytise Union initiatives to a wider public; in short, to collude in the formation of a European political system. Monetary Union provides examples. To maintain market credibility, governments have had to share control of the initiative with the Committee of Central Governors of the EU, which has, in turn, developed as an 'epistemic community' of convergent professional commitments, not least to a European *Ordnungspolitik* in which a stable monetary order is given independently of governments. (Dyson, 1994). More recently, the member states have agreed an expensive campaign to sell the single currency for fear of the deep political embarrassment that would flow from any public resistance to its use. So, not only may it be plausible to anticipate forms of European solidarity being constructed in the face of national government preferences to preserve a monopoly of identity formation; but, most ironically of all, it may be possible to envisage that identity being constructed by national authorities themselves. A further reason for this is the theme that we stress throughout this book: national governments may find it difficult to sustain a European policy framework that is not legitimated according to the same principles of liberal democracy that they use to justify power relations in other contexts.

2. Constitutional patriotism

Construction of a new European identity obviously begs the question 'constructed around what?' In this section we make the case for shared civic values forming the building blocks. Rather than treat this as a school of thought that can be attributed to any one author, we will attempt to distil the reflections of several. (Howe, 1995, 1997; Weiler *et al.*, 1995, 1997b; Habermas, 1996). The philosopher Ludwig Wittgenstein once argued that people should employ certain intellectual constructs in the same way as a man might climb up into a first-floor window only to throw away the ladder after he had reached his goal. Ethno-cultural homogeneity may have been an important ladder to nationhood, ethnically defined nationhood may have been a useful ladder to liberal democracy and well-established national communities may be surprisingly valuable ladders to European integration. However, none of this means that European identity formation needs to be restricted to patterns from the past and that it cannot, in contrast, involve a selective discarding of ladders. Liberal-democratic values, it is suggested, now have a force and embeddedness that allows them to be decoupled from the particularities of the nation state and universalised to transnational institutions constructed from societies that share those value commitments. Indeed, European publics may now be more likely to find a failure to do this anomalous, and incompatible with an increasingly ubiquitous assumption that all public power should indeed be democratic, than they are to accept that democracy needs be a nation-bound activity.

Meanwhile, there are, it is suggested, some very good reasons why European nations should 'externalise' some of their internally generated civic values as a means of disciplining themselves in their own enlightened self-interest. Jürgen Habermas argues that all solidarities will need to shift away from exclusivist ethno-cultural constructs as societies become more multicultural. And even majorities are likely to question ascriptive forms of identity that are 'given independently of the will formation of the citizens them-selves' (Habermas, 1996: 289). In contrast, people may come to identify with the EU, not because there is much substantive belief attached to being a member of the Union, but because it provides a kind of infrastructure by which all the other attachments they value with far more emotional force (local, national, gender, sexual, occupational and so on) can be managed and prevented from coming into excessive conflict with one another. The more identities become complex and over-lapping, the more something like the EU will be needed to play such a role.

In similar vein, Joseph Weiler points to a series of boundary abuses to which unconstrained nation identities have often been prone: those between territorially-defined nations; the state and the nation; and the nation and the individual. Far from supra-national disciplines being an act of self-denial, they are, in Weiler's view, a means of ensuring that the positive and creative aspects of nationhood are accentuated at the expense of the deformatory. Less concerned than Habermas to hollow out the ethnic character of national identity, he even suggests that the nations of Europe could draw their identity, in part, from ethno-cultural sources, while the Union concentrates its identity on civic values. Under such conditions nation and Union would not compete for exactly the same kind of citizen loyalty, and their identities could be made to serve different and mutually reinforcing functions, so increasing the chances of stable co-existence (Weiler, 1997a: 272). Such an identity based on a shared commitment to civic values would be a forward looking one to the extent that liberal democracy is not yet fully embodied in Union institutions, in the societies that may one day be brought into an enlarged Union, or, indeed, in all aspects of the existing member states.

One problem with all of this concerns the capacity of the Union to generate the requisite shared values and then to institutionalise them. We might agree that a 'demos' can be constructed without an 'ethnos' and that a political system can be regarded as legit-imate without it being a state. But it is far harder to accept that there can be a constitutional patriotism without a constitution.

Indeed, as stated in our introduction, an attempt to base Union identity on shared liberal-democratic values will only throw its own democratic deficit into sharp relief; and, although attempts to define a Union citizenship are not without substance, these entitlements sometimes struggle to attain a universal and even application without which they are somewhat devalued as institutionalised expressions of shared civic values. Examples of this are by no means limited to Britain's refusal to adopt the Social chapter of the Maastricht Treaty between 1993-7. The right of Union citizens to stand and vote in local and European elections if normally resident in another member state has come up against the objection that French mayors are responsible for the local police force (and that they ought, therefore, to continue to be French nationals) and, more recently, an attempt by Flemish communes of Brussels to introduce a language qualification to prevent non-Belgian voters upsetting the delicate balance between the local communities. It has also been difficult thus far for the Union to agree a forward-looking constitutional patriotism except in the vaguest of terms. Formulations such as 'political union' or 'ever closer union' have often been coined precisely so that they can be accepted by actors with incompatible motives. For example, Margaret Thatcher subscribed to the Single European Act (1986) only to argue within two years that if there was a teleology to European integration it had already been reached! In any case, it would probably be undesirable for the Union to be any more precise in its prescription of goals: to start legislating in advance for future generations, would be to destroy the 'open society' approaches that are important to various of the EU's other claims to political legitimacy. A further problem is that forward-looking identities are rarely free-standing: for them to command any authenticity they must either have some purchase over some historically experienced collectivity or have roots in what we have called the performance criteria of legitimation.

3. In praise of 'thin identity'

Because the most likely candidates for a Union based on shared civic values are liberal democracy and a supranational taming of the nation state, another possible objection to constitutional patriotism is that it would collapse identity into our other two categories of legitimacy – popular sovereignty and performance. There would, according to this point of view, no longer be a 'we-feeling' that existed independently of the outputs and procedures of the political system itself. Such a Union might also find it difficult to resolve boundary problems, as attachment to democracy is hardly unique to its member states and citizens, nor is commitment to supranationalism universal amongst them. One answer to this is that values can be endogenously formed and reinforced *within* political systems. Another is to argue that there are new forms of identity that emanate from wider sociological trends than any directly concerned with the political system itself (Bauman, 1997); and, moreover, that a constitutional patriotism of shared civic values is precisely the kind of solidarity one would expect to emerge from social contexts of this kind. To explain what is entailed let us begin by reviewing some of the things that have been said on the subject of 'thin identity'. Ernest Gellner somewhat playfully suggests that the modern citizen needs to be as 'modular' as possible: to be able to adjust to a remarkable variety of situations, to combine into many different associations and form relationships across all cultural categories. This presupposes an identity based on 'shared idiom', rather than 'pre-judged' loyalties and beliefs (Gellner, 1994). Anthony Giddens makes the like argument that we have failed to understand the extent to which solidarities in the modern world come from 'trust in abstract systems'. Collective action is no longer sustained by the things that go to make up *völkisch* identities – face to face interactions with those we would recognise as 'one of us'. Instead, we have little alternative to cohering in the modern world through our 'faith in shared impersonal principles' that allow us to deal at enormous distances with those we may never see. Traditional identities may persist but they 'can no longer be defended in a traditional way': to believe otherwise, is to prefer a lonely fundamentalism to flexible interaction (Giddens, 1996). Both authors regard this idiom of trust, communication and commitment to dialogue as amounting to a sense of identity that demarcates those who are prepared to play the game from those who are not: as Gellner puts it, subscribers to the 'thin identity' become capable of 'undertaking and honouring, and deeply internalising commitments and obligations by a single and sober act' (Gellner, 1994: 103). Giddens, on the other hand, emphasises the extent to which thin identities may be built around rituals of disclosure and standardised confidence building measures: even those who are unknown to one another can recognise their common identity by the manner in which they introduce themselves to one another. They can also produce communities of those who are prepared to open themselves to critical comparison, mutual justification and reflexive adaptation. So, in sum, there would seem to be an approach to identity that has more to do with the methods by which people deal with one another than with innate personal characteristics. It is also characterised by a certain attitude to identity itself: identity is seen as something that is open, changeable, even negotiable and inherently complex. Its holders are self-critical and, although they will often be unable to avoid conflicts between the different claims on their loyalties, they are committed to cultivating their identities over time in such a way as to reduce the probability of this happening. And, to reiterate, it is an approach to identity that is reproduced by individuals and societies as much as by political systems.

One recent study has concluded that there is, indeed, a 'presumption of trust' in contemporary international politics but no clear means of stabilising it (Rengger, 1997: 469). In contrast, the EU may be just the kind of political site that is needed to generate and stabilise 'thin identity'. Many of the features mentioned in the previous paragraph – elaborate normative codes, ritualistic disclosure, obligations of mutual justification and dense systems of communication – are conspicuously present in Union structures (Risse-Kappen, 1996: 68–71). What is more, the EU is a system of 'nested games': it gains strength from the fact that an enormous number of issues and initiatives are handled in the single political order, with the result that obligations tend to be cumulative and any cheating on one issue can ramify across all others at heavy and unpredictable cost to a player's reputation (Tsebelis: 1990). To continue with the jargon, the EU also operates under a 'heavy shadow of the future': in other words, participants know that they will have little choice but to work together for as long as they can foresee (H.Wallace in Wallace and Wallace, 1996). Of special interest to the idea of thin identity are two further features. First, the Union has been characterised as a 'negotiated order': although the rules are clear at any one time, they always leave room for renegotiation (Smith, 1996). So, in complete contrast to ascriptive and static identities, the EU may have a capacity to produce solidarities that are acceptable precisely because they are changeable and 'reflexively defined'. Second, the EU 'opens all to the search light of comparisons'. Weiler argues that this shifts the whole politics of identity in a 'critical' and 'Kantian' direction in which norms are not just followed but followed because individuals

Table 2.1 Measures of European identity

	Aus	Bel	Dk	Fr	Fin	Ger	Gr	Ire	It	Lx	Nl	Por	Sp	Sw	UK	Ave
Q1 'Please tell me whether you feel attached to the following?', Europinion, 9, 1996.																
Town	90	75	86	81	84	86	89	85	86	77	73	78	89	82	79	84
Region	93	78	88	82	76	87	86	83	85	82	72	79	91	85	81	84
Country	94	82	99	92	95	87	96	96	93	92	89	88	89	93	89	90
EU	69	67	72	61	61	70	42	50	70	78	67	36	50	58	43	63
Q2 In the near future do you feel yourself as ... ?, Eurobarometer 42, 1995.																
Nation only	–	29	48	22	–	29	46	38	25	17	33	41	34	–	49	33
Nation + EU	–	42	44	52	–	43	48	50	55	51	50	49	51	–	34	46
EU + Nation	–	14	4	12	–	15	4	6	12	13	9	4	5	–	7	10
EU only	–	10	3	11	–	9	2	3	4	12	6	3	–	–	7	7
Q3 Do you believe a) that countries should not have to submit to majority decisions, b) that the majority of countries should decide on some matters, Eurobarometer 42, 1995.																
a)	–	32	49	38	–	33	31	47	35	22	34	45	37	–	46	38
b)	–	35	34	37	–	42	39	28	38	56	49	23	30	–	29	36

can justify them to themselves (Weiler, 1997b: 268). One further consequence of this more adaptive and thoughtful approach to identity formation is that clashes between national and European solidarities may be easier to avoid, at least amongst those who start from a feeling of some commitment to both.

Where are we now?

The suggestions for possible routes to European identity formation made in the previous section are largely prescriptive and prognostic in character. Yet they are also given support by the many empirical studies that have been made of *existing* patterns of identity, of which Table 2.1 is typical. It confirms that even if we focus only on the territorial (as opposed to the cultural) dimension, many of those who live in the European Union have a multi-tiered sense of belonging. Of the tiers, the European remains, however, the weakest. As late as the 1970s, one study cast doubt on whether it had any significance at all, as there was little difference between the preparedness of respondents to identify with Europe and with humanity or the world as a whole (Duchesne and Frognier, 1995: 196). On the other hand, in many parts of the Union, subnational identifications with towns and regions are often as important as national ones, and many studies suggest that the multiple tiers of identity in Western Europe tend to be cumulative and mutually reinforcing, rather than contradictory. In particular, national identity would seem to function as the 'springboard and not the gravedigger of European identity' (Inglehart, 1977). Given the dependence of the Union on the intermediating institutions of domestic politics, this is not altogether surprising. Yet, choices may have to be made, and surveys that begin to probe how publics might trade off the claims of national and European attachments in the event of conflict are, therefore, especially useful. The second question in Table 2.1 (Q2) shows that more respondents feel themselves to be 'national and European' than 'European and national'; and the third (Q3) tests the crucial link between identity and the possibility of a transnational democratic polity by asking whether majorities of the whole should be regarded as more authoritative than those established in each of the EU's domestic arenas. It finds that, on average, the Union's public is evenly poised between the two possibilities. There are, however, significant variations between member states (Germany, The Netherlands and Luxembourg showing a preference for Union majoritarianism; Denmark, Greece, Ireland, Portugal and the UK for domestic majoritarianism; and the rest evenly divided). Another survey also indicates that support for Union majoritarianism in general falls when respondents are specifically asked whether their own country should be subject to more majority voting (Europinion, 1997: No 11)!

Turning to factors that may explain identification and support for the European Union, there is some disagreement between studies and an irritating tendency for a relationship that seems to hold in one period or location to break down in another. Nonetheless, there are a few straws in the wind that may be useful to our analysis, such as the following, principally drawn from Oskar Niedermayer and Richard Sinnott's contribution to the 'beliefs in Government' series:

- The growth of support and identification with the EU would seem to be more closely linked to the mere passage of time than to material benefits of integration. This suggests that the link between the performance and identity aspects of legitimacy may be relatively weak, contrary to the hypothesis that the one would tend to spill over to the other. On the other hand, political social-isation, learning and habituation – a feeling that the Union is a given part of the political landscape in much the same way as the nation – would seem to play a role. As Inglehart puts it, 'to some extent a polity may attain legitimacy as time goes by simply because it becomes familiar, part of the normal order of things' (Inglehart, 1977: 164).
- There would seem to be an important role for political leader-ship. Members of the public show a significant propensity to allow their views on European integration to be affected by national governments or the party programmes of the domestic parties they support. We will return to this in a moment.
- One consequence of learning and habituation is that over time different social strata tend to become more convergent in their attitudes to European integration. This is true of age cohorts, economic classes and supporters of different party political fam-ilies. This would seem to suggest that where Union membership is internally divisive it is not primarily because it aggravates pre-existing conflicts in member societies; rather, it is because the very choice between intergovernmental and supranational integration – as articulated by local political leaderships – opens up a new source of political cleavage.

■ One feature of European integration that is relatively resistant to other ups and downs would seem to be a fairly steady growth in trust. Although inhabitants of EU countries have not achieved a sense of trust for one another that matches that for other members of their own national community, there has been a steady erosion of the gap between the two. One study uses Eurobarometer data to compute a scale of trust from 0 to 3: trust of other EU nationalities is shown as growing from 1.55 to 1.75 on this scale between 1976 and 1990, compared with a steady level of 2.25 between members of the same national community (Niedermayer and Sinnott, 1995: 237). A role for the growth of trust in the formation of supranational identity could also explain why strong national identities need not conflict with the development of European ones. For, both may depend on what Inglehart has termed cognitive mobilisation: the capacity of publics to understand – and put their confidence – in highly aggregated and somewhat remote political systems. (Inglehart, 1970; 1977: 160) If true, all of this would bode well for notions of 'thin identity'.

■ Other possible indicators of a sense of solidarity are, first, that the public seem to have a stronger presumption than many of their governments that Union countries should move towards integration as a bloc and avoid groupings of flexible memberships (Europinion, 1997: 10) and, second, that Union publics seem to be evenly divided in their support for the removal of boundaries, even though this is an act that is highly symbolic in its acceptance of diminished national separateness. It is also something that, once again, requires a high level of trust in others (Europinion, 1996: 9).

Different interactions between the national and European levels

So far we have been considering interactions between national identities (collectively defined) and European identity formation at a general level. However, we need to consider the further possibility that individual national identities may interact differently with the EU in a manner that affects the legitimacy of the whole. Such differences may not be random, but may depend on particular *types* of state or nationhood. Here a number of hypotheses suggest themselves for examination.

Forms of national identity

At first sight it seems plausible to suppose that congruity between the national and European levels of identity would depend on whether national identity is predominantly ethnic (*völkisch*) or civic (*Verfassungspatriotismus*) in character. However, the example of Germany suggests that it is possible for carriers of a *völkisch* identity to accept European integration as a valuable discipline on the excesses of ethnicity and as something that is not regarded as a threat, precisely because it is grounded in shared values, rather than aspirations to ethno-cultural homogeneity. The example of France, on the other hand, would suggest that it is possible for those whose national pride is already closely wrapped up with civic ideals to identity with the EU on the basis that it is an externalisation of some of those values. In his last Presidential broadcast, François Mitterrand, urged his compatriots not to 'separate the glory of France from the European construction'. Less important than whether it falls into the ethnic or civic category is the kind of boundary relationship implied by different concepts of national identity. The key question is whether it is easily adapted to the notion of pooling sovereignty, or involvement with others in some kind of collectively binding decision process. It is precisely because British national identity is, for historical reasons, so heavily wrapped up with the notion of the absolute and inalienable sovereignty of the Westminster Parliament, that it is so hard to accommodate with anything more than intergovernmental models of European cooperation.

Another fascinating illustration of how important it is for shared authority to be regarded as an opportunity, rather than a threat to identity, is provided by the growth of collaborative agreements between boundary regions of different member states. In some cases, these have been regarded as helping member states adapt to the porosity of frontiers and the interpenetration of economic interests amongst their peripheral regions, not to mention the sometimes complex ethno-cultural characteristics of such areas. Proposals for inter-regional agreements between Alsace-Lorraine, North Rhine-Westphalia, Luxembourg and Francophone Belgium, or between

The Netherlands, Flanders and the Pas de Calais, have, accordingly, only provoked arguments about who should be excluded, rather than disputes about whether such initiatives should happen at all. In other cases, however, they have been seen as threatening. A recent attempt to strengthen inter-regional collaboration between the northern most *Land* of Germany and southern Denmark produced a protest in which Danes – each carrying a national flag – formed a human chain the length of the national boundary. As with the British case, Danish identity has been closely constructed around the idea of protecting the national territory against foreign invasion.

Large and small states

It is possible that people who live in small states are more aware of the limited capacity of their governments to ensure physical protection, economic performance and welfare entitlements. For these essentially performance related reasons, they may be readier to identify with a European Union that is capable of providing valuable state supplementing roles. Inhabitants of smaller states may also have reason to prefer a supranational approach to European integration in which decisions are made by impartial institutions to an intergovernmental one in which large states are likely to dominate. Delors has thus justified Union action on the grounds that 'when the European construction stagnates, the relative weight of nations makes itself felt. When it works well, each country is treated by the others with attention regardless of its demographic, political or economic importance' (Delors, 1994: 226). Considerations such as these may explain high levels of support for an ambitiously conceived Union in Belgium, Ireland, Luxembourg and The Netherlands. However, the Scandinavian countries, which are also small in terms of population, provide instances of small states where European integration is viewed with some suspicion. One reason for this is that the limited capacity of small states may be counterbalanced by their intimacy as political arenas: the ratio between those making collective decisions and those on the receiving end of government (Sartori, 1988: 215) deteriorates particularly badly as powers gravitate from small state politics to EU institutions. Perceptions of whether a country is part of the core or the periphery of the EU's political system also have to be taken into account. These may be governed by geography (distance from Brussels) or history (length of membership), though neither seems to have had particularly deleterious effects on support for the EU in Finland, Ireland or Portugal. Nor do the large states show any uniformity in the extent to which their publics have developed feelings of European identity. We clearly need to turn to other factors to explain different levels of identification across national arenas.

Divided national communities and European integration

A further possibility is that European identity will be stronger where states have been relatively less successful in capturing sentiments of political loyalty for the nation. This would suggest that support for European integration will be greater amongst the more internally divided of the member states, amongst minority communities, in peripheral regions and in countries where state formation has in some sense been imperfect. Belgium – with a 60:40 divide between two different ethno-linguistic communities (Flanders and Wallonia) – is the most internally divided of the EU countries and also one of the most Euro-enthusiastic. Likewise, high levels of support for the Union in Italy are often linked to the failure of the state to secure universal acceptance for its legitimacy across all regions and social segments. And, during the period 1949–1989, West German support for European integration was often linked to the difficulties of identifying with a divided state of uncertain status. It is also significant that support for European integration is higher than the national average in Scotland and Wales in the UK and in the Basque and Catalan regions of Spain. However, in other cases, such as Northern Ireland, where the Unionist majority opposed British entry to the European Community (Lord, 1993), contending attitudes towards European integration may interact less benignly into sub-regional hostilities, with alignments being affected by relative interests in the softening or hardening of boundaries between national identities. Indeed, the idea that holders of problematic national identities are more likely to support European integration sits uncomfortably with earlier evidence that 'integration into the national system is a precondition for becoming a good citizen of Europe' (Martinotti and Stefanizzi in Niedermayer and Sinnott, 1995: 163) and that 'integrating units must themselves be integrated political communities'.

52

European Integration and histories of state failure

Another possibility is that identification with the EU is linked to different histories of state success and failure. The most obvious way in which a state can fail to protect its citizens is in war, and there would seem to be some link between different experiences of international conflict in the twentieth century and attitudes towards European integration. The original Six – France, Germany, Italy and the Benelux – were all countries that had at some point been defeated, occupied or implicated in the crimes of the Second World War. In contrast, Britain, which had in many ways been a socially divided country before 1939, emerged from the conflict with renewed confidence in its internal social solidarity and international survival skills. However, the relationship between perceptions of state success and failure and the direction of policy expectations towards the European arena may be associated with more prosaic considerations of economic performance. This would, for example, explain the renewed interest that France showed in European integration after the failure of 'Mitterrand experiment' of 1981–3. But it would not so readily explain why support for European integration has not declined in Germany in spite of marked improvements in national economic performance since the 1950s.

National elite support

The foregoing hypotheses are suggestive rather than decisive. The precise relationship between national and European identities is a product of many factors, rather than of any one in isolation. In addition, these structural-historical factors have to be mediated through different patterns of elite support for European integration. It is not just that public attitudes towards integration show evidence of high susceptibility to political leadership by local elites, reflecting low levels of socialisation into an unfamiliar political system. It is also that the nation state is in a permanent state of construction and reconstruction in parallel with that of the Union itself. This means that national elites have to form a view as to how they would like the two identities to interact, though, they will, of course, differ in their relative capacity to deliver their objectives and in their willingness to expend resources to that end. In an early work, Moravcsik suggests that domestic elites may come under pressure to promote compatibility between national

Table 2.2 Cross-country comparison of elite attitudes to EU. Top Decision-makers survey conducted February–May 1996, sample size 3788 (http://europa.eu.int/comm/dg10/eb-top/en)

	Do you think the EU is a good thing?	The Commission should resign where it does not have the support of a majority of the EP	In EU legislation, taxation and expenditure the EP should have equal rights with the Council	The EU should have a government responsible to the EP
Germany	97	89 (+6)	73 (+10)	72 (+7)
Spain	97	84 (+1)	64 (+1)	77 (+12)
Italy	97	91 (+8)	71 (+8)	87 (+22)
Belgium	96	90 (+7)	78 (+15)	89 (+24)
Ireland	96	62 (−21)	50 (−13)	40 (−25)
The Netherlands	96	91 (+8)	61 (−2)	63 (−2)
Finland	94	66 (−17)	24 (−39)	25 (−40)
France	93	84 (+1)	59 (−4)	64 (−1)
Luxembourg	93	79 (−4)	46	52
Greece	92	91 (+8)	77 (+14)	72 (+7)
Portugal	91	67 (−16)	45 (−18)	33 (−32)
Austria	90	84 (+1)	57 (−6)	65 0
UK	86	69 (−14)	53 (−10)	43 (−22)
Denmark	84	55 (−28)	23 (−40)	16 (−49)
Sweden	84	63 (−20)	37 (−26)	36 (29)
Average	94	83	63	65

and European identities: all governments are constrained to play a two level game in which they have to find solutions that are viable in both domestic and European bargaining; those who are excessively inhibited by domestic constraints, may grow tired of 'losing the game' at European level and seek to restructure their internal politics (Moravcsik, 1989: 25).

On the other hand, national elites may tend to be conservative, rather than creative elements in the politics of identity. They recruit in their own image, invest their careers in a settled institutional order and often frame their understanding of problems by means of 'standard operating assumptions' etched deep in the collective memories of the domestic organisations to which they belong (government departments, parties, parliaments and so on) (March and Olson, 1984). All of this would seem to make national elites unlikely entrepreneurs for European integration, until it is remembered that they may need European frameworks to achieve other objectives; that certain kinds of commitment to the Union may enter the institutional conservatism of domestic politics in their own right; and that particular political leaders may be motivated by seering personal experiences to challenge or circumvent the standard operating assumptions of domestic bureaucracies. On the last point, it is difficult to understand the Schuman Plan without the biographical details of Jean Monnet and Robert Schuman (Monnet, 1976; Poidevin, 1986) or Monetary Union without the personal value commitments Hans-Dietrich Genscher and Helmut Kohl (Dyson, 1994). On the penultimate point, there is evidence that national elites are consistently more likely than their publics to support the need for some kind of European Union. Where they differ across countries is in their concepts of how a Union would be most legitimately constructed. Some of these contrasts are brought out in Table 2.2, with figures in brackets showing how preferences on questions of institutional choice deviate from average either in a supranational direction (+) or an intergovernmental one (−).

Implications for the shape of the EU's political system

Finally, we need to consider the connection between a European identity and the character of the EU's political system. This connection seems to be a strongly circular one: the politics of identity shape the EU's political system and the EU's political system has its own consequences for patterns of European identity. Whatever the long term prospects, most students of integration would probably agree that the development of the Union has had to start from a relatively weak and contested sense of European identity. The need to secure some legitimacy and effectiveness in spite of this difficulty has, in turn, been responsible for some of the principal characteristics of Union power relations. We now reflect cursorily on these, in part as a link to subsequent chapters on democracy, performance and legitimacy in the EU.

One response may have been for the Union to concentrate on those functions of government that require only a weak sense of solidarity. Thus Majone argues that the EU has developed as a 'fourth branch of government' that is mainly focused on regulation, as other forms of governance – economic stabilisation or redistribution – would require higher levels of active public compliance and a more explicit role in distributing political values between states and social groups. The obvious difficulty is whether this is a sustainable pattern of policy allocation and demarcation. Fritz Scharpf has pointed out that pressure on the Union to do more to sustain the welfare state could, in combination with Monetary Union, push it towards precisely the opposite ranking of priorities to that anticipated by Majone: in other words, redistribution, stabilisation and regulation (Scharpf, 1997). Indeed, even if the EU has been focused in terms of governmental functions, it has scarcely been so in the range of issue areas that it has had to bring within its ambit. Wessels points out that all the normal issues covered by domestic governments (with the possible exception of external physical security) are now part of the EU's formal responsibility (Wessels, 1997: 278).

If the EU has not been able to get away with a light load, has it been able to resolve its identity and legitimacy difficulties by adopting a 'light touch'? To a certain extent it has. For example, the use of the directive as the principal legislative instrument is important here, as it defines a target and leaves it to the addressee (usually a member government) to decide precisely how that goal is to be reached. Likewise the use of the principle of mutual recognition short-circuited any need to harmonise the product standards of all twelve member states and replaced it with the presumption that a standard that was good enough for one country was good enough for all. However, even arrangements such as these do not remove an impression that the Union often makes heavy demands on the cooperation and patience of all kinds of actors: its legislative output at times approaches that of national governments; a tendency for national governments to offload some of their problems may mean that it has to cope with questions that require more, and not less, political legitimacy; and some of the decisions it has to take involve 'concentrated' rather than 'diffuse' interests, with the result that they are highly visible and impact strongly on the life chances of social groups. Fishing and other agricultural policies are obvious examples.

Given that it may not always be able to avoid a heavy load or a heavy hand, the EU has had to look to two forms of political incorporation to soften legitimacy problems presented by low European identification: by building national governments into its own political system its acts may appear to be those of domestic authorities to whom the legitimating force of national identities are available; by implicating organised non-governmental actors in policy formulation and implementation, it can ensure that those who are most immediately and intensively affected by its policy outputs are bound in by their participation and consent. On the first aspect, Wolfgang Wessels has recently estimated that around 40 per cent of senior German civil servants are now involved in EU decision-making processes, and that a high proportion of the EU's allocative decisions are delivered through the adjustment of national budgets and regulations to policies that have been agreed – or just discussed – at the Union level (Wessels, 1997: 278, 280). On the second aspect, standing technical committees involving sub-national actors play a key role in policy development (Greenwood, 1997). On the other hand, neither of these forms of political incorporation is without its problems: what may be intended as stop-gaps for the fuller development of European identity and democracy may themselves complicate the transition to a more legitimate polity.

Conclusion

If the key issue of identity is its contribution to the trust necessary between people for democratic procedures to work, then our analysis has suggested a number of different ways in which this trust might be attained at the European level. One is to limit the range of issues, or the degree of 'touch' for Euro decision-making, so that it need not put too much strain on loyalty. This might be called the negative approach, and it obviously has its limits. More positively there is the prospect of a form of identity based on citizenship, and the guarantee of basic civil and economic rights which would be immune from erosion by contingent majorities. Then there is the idea of a 'thin identity' which would provide the framework for a pluralism of other identities, including the national one, within a European umbrella. Arguably these last two are now much more appropriate forms of political identity for the contemporary world than the 'ethnic' identities and loyalties of the past, though they may require a greater sophistication among electorates, and a certain restraint among political elites, if they are still not to be vulnerable to the appeal of more primordial loyalties in times of crisis. To the extent that shared civic values are a part of any appropriate solution, identity formation will require the democratisation of the Union, as well as vice versa. It is to the problem of providing the Union with democratic legitimacy that we now turn.

CHAPTER THREE

Democracy

Introduction

We have argued that popular sovereignty is the appropriate test of the EU's legitimacy, as the Union exercises its powers over societies that have grown accustomed to measuring the rightfulness of political authority by liberal democratic values. The obvious difficulties this raises can be posed as questions that correspond to the two halves of the term 'popular sovereignty'. Are those who live in the EU a 'people'? And is it possible to construct institutions by which they can be meaningfully 'sovereign' at the Union level? We tackled the first of these questions in the previous chapter where we concluded that any European identity would at best have to be constructed idiosyncratically and that this would restrict possibilities for the development of the Union's political system, including its democratic institutions. The second question is the subject of this chapter. We begin by positing two models. Under an *intergovernmental* approach, national democracies are adapted to the task of legitimating the Union, with national parliaments and electorates ratifying, and periodically up-dating, the Treaties, as well as forming and dismissing the governments that make up the European Council and Council of Ministers. Under a *supranational* approach, the EU develops a democracy of its own, in which a pan-European electorate and parliament has important powers over the Union's leadership. Table 3.1 summarises these differences. Although it presents the models as 'ideal types', we will see that some features of both have already been mixed and matched in present EU institutions.

Now, to anticipate our argument a little, we will show that neither of these models can, at this stage of the Union's development,

Table 3.1 **The legitimacy claims of intergovernmental and supranational approaches to the democratisation of the EU**

	Legitimacy claims of 2 models (Ideal type)		
	Best means of authorising political leadership	Best way of making EU governance representative	Best means of making EU governance accountable
Intergovernmental	CELL 1 Treaty ratifications Domestic election of members of European Council and Council of Ministers	CELL 2 Representation of national governments through Council and European Council National allocations of Commissioners and MEPs	CELL 3 Need for members of the European Council and Council of Ministers to account to national parliaments and electorates
Supranational	CELL 4 Direct or indirect election of Union's political leadership by entire EU electorate	CELL 5 An independent Commission with pan-European authorisation Directly elected European Parliament organised into ideological groupings	CELL 6 Need for Commission and Council to account to European Parliament and for this, in turn, to be accountable to entire European electorate

offer an unproblematic delivery of what we have identified as the legitimating qualities of democracy: the popular authorisation of political leadership, accountability of power holders to the public and representative government. In many ways, this is the core of the problem known as the 'democratic deficit' of the EU; for, together, the two models exhaust the most obvious routes by which the Union can be democratised. Needless to say, things are further complicated because there are good reasons to believe that the relative legitimacy of intergovernmental and supranational approaches will play differently across the national sub-arenas of the Union. The first and second parts of this chapter examine the problems with delivering democratic legitimation by intergovernmental and supranational means respectively. The third part of this chapter will elaborate the reasons why the national arenas of the EU may find it hard to accept a single set of solutions to the challenge of democratic legitimation at Union level. The fourth part will explore the consequences of our analysis for EU power relations, the shape of the Union's political system and the character of such democratic politics as are practised at European level.

The Intergovernmental model: can the EU be democratised through its member states?

Authorisation of power under the intergovernmental model

As shown in the first cell of Table 3.1, intergovernmentalists might suggest that the best way of conferring democratic legitimacy on the Union would be through the ratification of EU Treaties by the democratic institutions of each member state and the election of national governments, whose members then go on to serve on the European Council and Council of Ministers. The first can be seen as giving legitimacy to the basic structure of power relations at Union level, and the second as providing particular political leaderships with the right to make decisions in the EU.

Successive Union Treaties provide one possible source of democratic authorisation for the exercise of Union power, for they have to be ratified according to the democratic conventions of each member state: by referendum in some countries and by parliamentary vote in others. Some commentators even regard the Treaties as a proto-constitution that could one day be consolidated into a more systematic legitimation of power relations at the Union level, if only as an 'inventory' of existing arrangements (Weidenfeld, 1994: 11). But, for all its disjointed incrementalism, the present Treaty process may have advantages over some 'ideal moment' of consent giving through constitutionalisation. For, the frequency with which the Union has to revise its Treaties – to ensure that its competence, decision-rules and membership keep up with changing circumstances – hands important leverage to domestic democratic actors (Judge, 1995: 89).

On the other hand, even where domestic ratification of Union Treaty changes is frequent, it is not pre-programmed to occur at regular intervals. The Treaty process may also add substantial inertia to power relations in the EU. Very often the Union will be operating under grants of power that were not made by present generations but by the representatives of their parents and grand-parents. Even an initiative as recent as Monetary Union has raised some interesting questions about the right of one cohort of citizens to bind a slightly different one. In May 1997, the Swedish Government announced that it did not feel itself to have sufficient domestic consent to proceed with a single currency until this had been the subject of a further general election. This was coyness indeed, given that an automatic transition to Monetary Union had been approved by universal adult suffrage under the terms of the referendum on Swedish entry to the Union just two and a half years earlier (*Financial Times*, 29 May, 1997).

In any case, the Treaties are only partially constitutive of power relations at the Union level. Although they define decision rules and adumbrate important policy regimes, the devil is in their sub-sequent application, and they leave a great deal of room for the exercise of discretionary political power. It is, therefore, as import-ant in the Union, as in any other political system, that individual political leaderships should be adequately authorised. Now the designers of the EU's institutions thought they had a very neat solution in this regard. By reserving final decisions on most matters of importance to the Council of Ministers, while providing the Commission with certain monopoly rights to make new proposals, it was hoped that the European Community would enjoy all the benefits of a supranational agenda-setter while drawing its demo-cratic authorisation from established national democracies. For, it was believed, the proposing body (the Commission) need not be elected so long as the deciding body (the Council) was made up of those who had been chosen by the people. The need to construct a Euro-democracy would apparently be short-circuited, and the Union could justifiably demand that all its member states be democ-racies without itself being a democracy. Let us call this *domestic authorisation*, to drive home the point that democratic consent to Union decisions is seen as being channelled through national elec-torates and parliaments to the Council of Ministers. It is crucial to our analysis. For, it was a key assumption on which the Union was constructed for at least the first forty years of its existence, and, to the extent that there continue to be shortcomings in present arrangements for the European Parliament to confirm the Commission in office, it remains central even to the legitimacy claims of the contemporary Union. It is, additionally, the kind of argument on which intergovernmentalists need to rely if they are to defend present arrangements against those who advocate a more supranational pattern of democratic authorisation, or those who doubt that it can ever be right to have any element of executive authority at European level.

One obvious problem with domestic authorisation is that the national governments who make up the EU's Council of Ministers are only individually elected in the domestic arena, and not collectively authorised to act at Union level. This is a crucial distinction. For, the Council of Ministers is far more than the sum of its individual parts. As the first President of the Commission, Walter Hallstein, put it, 'the Council is not a conference of governments but an institution of the Community' (Hallstein, 1970: 77). Majority voting – which allows governments to outvote one another – is now the norm. Indeed, the national veto may well have become a blunt instrument long before governments were prepared to admit this too openly to their publics (Teasdale, 1993).

'Informal majority voting' – whereby governments do not hold out once they realise they are in a minority – is widespread, as is the closely related process of consolidating bargains into elaborate package deals that would not command unanimous consent for each of their component parts. There are also strong norms that shape the way in which consensus is formed, as well as a highly institutionalised process for taking and preparing decisions. A leading study of the Council estimates that 85 per cent of decisions are settled by national civil servants bargaining within the Council's technocracy and only around 15 per cent are decided by ministers themselves (Hayes-Renshaw and Wallace, 1996: 78). It is precisely by means of a collegiality that transcends the notion of concurrent consent by fifteen separately elected governments that the most intergovernmental parts of the Union – Common Foreign and Security Policy (CFSP: second pillar) and Justice and Home Affairs (JHA: third pillar) – are supposed to be capable of producing coherent and cumulative policies. One author writes of an *acquis politique* whereby a collective foreign policy tends to emerge through an accumulation of precedents and orientations (Ifestos, 1987). Such a sunk investment in consensus formation may, however, be profoundly constraining of some national democracies, and, worst of all, of some more than others.

Sometimes – informal majority voting and policy socialisation – represent honest but inadequate attempts to preserve the link between Council decisions and their indirect authorisation through national democracies. On other occasions they may be deliberately exploited to create a facade of unanimous consent, in the hope that this will head off the need for more explicit forms of democratic authorisation for EU power relations. For example, in 1985, the British Government designed and proposed an elaborate code of informal majority voting, in order to enact the Single Market programme without Treaty changes to Council decision-making rules or the powers of the European Parliament. One attraction of this course of action was that it would have avoided the need to submit potentially contentious legislation to the House of Commons (*Financial Times*, June 1985).

Another difficulty is that the Council is, in any case, only a part of the political leadership of the EU: there is also the Commission to consider. The notion that the Commission can piggy-back on the democratic authorisation of the Council, so long as it is the latter which makes the final decisions, seriously under-states the importance of agenda-setting as an independent source of political power. E.E. Schattsneider once described it as the power to determine what 'politics is all about' and B. Guy Peters has argued that the timing and 'exact social and political construction of the issue' go a long way to determining the substantive outcomes of EU policy making. (Schattsneider, 1960; Lukes, 1974; Peters, 1994; Peters, 1996). Both of the two most important economic initiatives undertaken by the Union in the last two decades – the Single Market and Monetary Union – provide striking examples. The former was based on a White Paper that was prepared at breakneck speed by just two Commissioners – Lord Cockfield and Jacques Delors himself – and presented with only ten days to spare before a meeting of the Heads of Government in the European Council. Yet, all but 18 of the initial 282 measures passed into law over the following seven years (Cockfield, 1994: 86). The explanation for this cannot be found in an overwhelming consensus of member governments – many of whose ideal preferences deviated from individual aspects of the programme or, indeed, from its overall deregulatory bias (Favier and Martin-Roland, 1991). The White Paper's almost unquestioned hegemony as a reference point for how the Single Market should be constructed rested, instead, on a belief that, if one government was to deviate too far from the positions of the independent agenda-setter, the whole project would sink under the weight of intergovernmental wrangling (Cockfield, 1994: 98). In the case of Monetary Union, the power of initiative was even sub-contracted one stage further than the Commission. National Central Bank Governors were allowed to draw up their own draft statute for a European Central Bank. Yet, in a striking illustration of the power of the agenda-setter, this passed, without amendment into a protocol to the Treaty of European Union (Dyson, 1994: 147).

In the case of the EU, the power of the agenda-setter is not just one over the imagination of others. In many areas, it consists of a formal Commission monopoly on the right to make new proposals. The fact that the Council can only act if it has received a proposal, and only deviate from such a proposal by unanimous vote, can be used by the Commission to put an arm-lock on the member states. As their interests become more entangled with the Union, the one thing that governments can often not afford is that no decision should be taken at all. As Beate Kohle-Koch puts it, 'with the deepening of integration, the costs of non-decisions increase to such an extent that most actors settle for a second to best solution rather than for no decision at all' (Kohler-Koch, 1996: 362). The beef crisis, for example, put the Major Government in the peculiar position of backing the Commission's role in any resolution of the stand-off between the UK and other member states. For, the price of non-decision was that the ban stayed.

To do full justice, however, to the idea of domestic authorisation of Union power through the Council of Ministers and the European Council, we need to consider the adequacy of one further argument. This is that it does not very much if the Commission has strong and independent powers of agenda-setting, so long as it acts within the terms of some 'agency', that is both conferred and withdrawable by representatives of its member democracies. The problem with this is that recent studies of the Commission's role in the EU's political system have tended to emphasise its capacity to outstrip the terms of any agency and establish substantial political autonomy of its own. Amongst reasons given for this are the following:

- Informational asymmetries make it hard for the Council to supervise the Commission. In contrast to national governments who are usually more than fully involved in their domestic politics, the Commission enjoys two kinds of advantage: permanent concentration on Union affairs and a position at the junction of all information sources that affect the operation of the Union. These factors, in turn, allow it to construct 'problems', 'solutions', and relationships between the two, in a manner that suits its own purposes (Pollack, 1997: 108).

- The Commission will have opportunities for political leadership where governments enter the European arena with partial or interdependent preferences; in other words, where they do not fully know what they want, or they are open to learning, or rational action depends crucially on what others intend to do (Risse-Kappen, 1996). In some cases, such as competition policy and forms of environmental regulation, the domestic policy of particular member states has even been derived from Commission proposals for new EU rules, in contradistinction to the normal, and implicitly more passive, view of the Union as being engaged in 'splitting the difference' between pre-existing national policy regimes.

- The Commission has the power to mobilise non-state actors into the European arena and form its own client relationships in a manner that constrains member governments (Hooghe, 1995: 177; H. Wallace in Wallace and Wallace, 1996: 53). It can even align with one section of a member government against another. By recruiting the twelve central bank governors on to the Delors Committee charged with examining options for a Monetary Union between the Hanover (June, 1988) and Madrid (June, 1989) European Councils, Delors was able to ensure the dominance of his own preferred option of a Single Currency managed by a European Central Bank (Dyson, 1994: 129–34). Another example is that national Environment ministers are often thought to align with the Commission against Economics departments in their own governments (Sbragia, 1996: 247).

- Decision-making rules may require member states to be unanimous if they are to rein back the Commission. Thus one important way in which the Commission can use its powers of initiative to create 'new equilibria' amongst the governments is to head off 'united fronts' against its own authority (Marks *et al.*, 1996: 354; Richardson, 1996: 272). This may, for example, have been very important in preserving the power of the Commission to limit national subsidies to domestic producers during the downturn in the European economy between 1992 and 1996. At different times, several member governments came under intense domestic pressure to defy the Commission: Germany over Volkswagen, France over Air France and Italy over its steel producers. However, at no point, were the conditions right for a simultaneous assault by all member states on the Commission's role; indeed, by exercising its powers aggressively, the Commission ensured that there would always be some member governments with an interest in a tough competition policy.

■ Member states develop dependencies of their own on a strong Commission. An independent arbiter may be needed to prevent arguments about 'sharing value' (cutting up the cake) swamping opportunities to 'create value' (enlargening the cake) (Sebenius, 1992). This, as we have seen, was the secret of the Commission's remarkable success in holding the member states to its own construction of the Single Market programme, even though there were few individual items in the package that did not attract opposition from at least one member state.

In short, the Commission may enjoy too many degrees of political freedom from national governments to sustain the notion that the Union's democratic legitimacy can be plausibly arranged through the connection of the Council to domestic electorates. To claw back the independence of the Commission might, on the other hand, undercut the performance of the Union, and even that of member states themselves. As performance is itself an important aspect of legitimacy, this leaves the option of domestic authorisation of Union power through the Council of Ministers and European Council in some considerable difficulty: the argument that it can ground some element of supranational power, so long as the Commission remains the agent of national democracies, has been found wanting; on the other hand, there are reasons to doubt the effectiveness of a pure form of intergovernmentalism that does not avail itself of some supranational supports in the performance of tasks at the European level. Whether, in contrast, supranational power holders can be adequately authorised by supranational democratic structures we will consider in a moment. First, however, we must look at representation and accountability, under intergovernmental approaches.

Representation under the intergovernmental model

Representation can be structured in a variety of ways, with dramatic consequences for the distribution of political values. Social choice theory shows that outcomes always depend on the method by which votes are added, not just on votes themselves (Arrow, 1963). Nor do representative institutions passively reflect preferences. They also shape and perpetuate values by the manner in which they structure dialogue and decision-making rules (Shepsle, 1989). Schattsneider once remarked that they mobilise bias (Schattsneider, 1960). Small wonder that the choice of representative system has often been a conflict-laden moment in the development of political systems: a classic example of how political change – and the substitution of one institutional order for another – tend to crystallise disputes about legitimacy (Graeger, 1994: 17–18). On the other hand, once notions of political legitimacy do become settled in any political system, they can go along way to resolve the indeterminacies of democratic representation: acceptable decision rules and methods of aggregation are just those that are best justified in terms of the shared values of the society in question. But all of this presents a chicken and egg problem for a new political system like the EU: an agreed concept of legitimacy is needed to stabilise a system of representation, yet a system of representation is needed to impart legitimacy.

Against this background, the intergovernmental answer that the public should be represented in the EU through domestic democratic processes (see cell 2 of Table 3.1) appears superficially attractive. Such a solution constitutes the smallest possible departure from pre-existing notions of representation; it avoids the contentious act of shoe-horning countries with conflicting norms of representation into a single democratic structure at the European level; and it has the important advantage of corresponding with the public's own views on how it ought to be represented in the European arena. A remarkable piece of evidence for this comes from the finding by *Eurobarometer* that most people continue to believe that MEPs should sit as national blocs, even though they come from widely diverse party political families and one of the arguments for having a European Parliament is that it can provide an element of transnational ideological representation to counterbalance the bias towards cultural-territorial representation inherent in the organisation of the Council.

An intergovernmental model of representation would ideally follow a consociational approach with the following features: publics would entrust their national elites with wide discretion to represent them at the European level; pay-offs from the political system would be proportional to national weights; agreements would depend on the concurrent consent of all member governments, though, of course, this could take the form of a 'diffuse reciprocation' that left room for majority voting on individual questions; and, above all, cultural-territorial segmentation would be respected with the implication that there would be some upper limit to political discourse and coalition building across national boundaries. In such a way, each member democracy would remain self-contained, free to adopt its own representative methods, and to authorise, or remove, in its own idiosyncratic fashion, those who attend EU institutions. European countries would be able to solve their collective action problems while remaining separate life worlds (Taylor, 1993; Chryssochou, 1994; Gabel, 1994).

Now, the one point on which this model is strong is that Union legitimacy would seem to be linked to proportionality in the treatment of member states. Painstaking attempts are made to embed proportionality in the EU's representative structures: each state receives an allocation of Commissioners, a chance to hold the rotating Presidency of the Council, a weighted allocation of votes and, in the party groups of the European Parliament, the D'Hondt system of proportionality between national party delegations is applied right down to the allocation of seats on committees and opportunities to bid for rapporteurships (Corbett et al, 1995). It is likewise possible to trace several policy regimes to the special concerns of particular member states and it is, arguably, where proportionality of pay-offs breaks down that the Union encounters some of its most serious legitimacy problems. Britain's early membership problems can, for example, be linked to a failure to find any equivalent for the UK of the 'elegant bargain' by which France received agricultural protection and Germany industrial free trade in the Treaty of Rome (Taylor, 1983: 299).

It is, however, doubtful whether consociational representation can be a sufficient solution at Union level. To see why, let us begin by observing that there is one very good structural reason why the Union's political agenda is likely to provoke alignments that cross-cut the national-territorial segmentation of the EU: the principle of subsidiarity enjoins the Union to concentrate precisely on those problems that spill across political boundaries. In such circum-stances, a monopoly of representation by national governments would tend to distort processes of democratic aggregation. For the idea that individuals should have just one vote to select a team of people to perform two functions – form the national government and then go on to represent them at Union level – breaks down where the public has good reasons for not wanting to align in the same way in the two arenas. Where people are open to learning and mutual persuasion there is even less justification for giving governments a monopoly on coalition-formation and debate, except, maybe, in cases where the communities are not just terri-torially segmented but bitterly divided to the point of not being on speaking terms. For, it is dialogue, debate and interaction between rulers and the ruled that provides much of the moral quality of representative systems of government. Public debate and consulta-tion are often important to the legitimacy of eventual decisions. As well as being a key stage in the formation of preferences, and in testing their validity, they often provide a convergence and simplification of decision, so reducing some of the troubling indeterminacies of representation that we discussed earlier (Held, 1993). In contrast, we have seen that consociational approaches presuppose a compartmentalisation of the Union debate along national lines. This may lead to a regrettable cartelisation of politics in which national governments have a monopoly of decisions at the Union level, which is, in turn, used to reinforce a privileged position in domestic affairs. For governments can attempt to assign policies between the arenas according to their estimate of where they are most likely to get their way, exploit information gaps between the two levels and confront publics and parliaments with Union decisions that are *faits accomplis.*

Arguably, it was precisely such a consociational pattern of negotiation – with its emphasis on the need to trust national elites – that was delegitimised by the Maastricht ratification crisis. Jacques Delors has, accordingly, argued that the problem with democracy in the European Union is not the insufficient incorporation of national governments into the Union's political system, but the inadequate incorporation of the Union into the domestic politics of member societies (Delors, 1994: 225) A political system that is coming to rely on direct public cooperation to the extent of the Union – if only to handle periodic ratifications of Treaty changes – needs its own resources of public persuasion. It cannot, therefore, be expected to perform to the required standards under a consociational model of democratic representation.

Accountability under the intergovernmental model

As shown in cell 3 of Table 3.1, democratic accountability is best arranged under the intergovernmental model where national parliaments hold their governments responsible for their decisions on the Council of Ministers, and voters use national elections as a check on the handling of EU issues by their own government and parliament. Now, recent years have seen some interesting developments in this 'domestic accountability model'. Before the Single Act and the Treaty of European Union, only the Danish Parliament came close to indicating the positions that it would like its government to adopt on new EU legislation. Since then, almost all national parliaments have taken measures to strengthen control. The German Bundestag claims to have obliged the Federal Government to inform it of its voting intentions in the Council, and the Dutch Parliament requires ministers to discuss annotated agendas of forthcoming Council meetings with its European affairs committee. The Italian Senate has begun to debate six monthly Presidency programmes. The Spanish Cortes has found it is useful to know the position of each member state, so that it can review negotiating tactics and coalition formation, as well as the ideal positions of its own government (Round Table on the Roles of the European Parliament and National Parliaments: European Parliament, Brussels, 16–17 April, 1997). The French Assembly has even secured some rights of initiative on EU matters that it does not possess in domestic politics (Judge, 1995: 91). A convention has developed that draft legislation should be sent to national parliaments six weeks before a vote is taken in the Council and the Amsterdam Treaty attempts to formalise this arrangement. Through the COSAC network, national Parliaments have also linked up with one another, and the European Parliament, to exchange information and assessments. At the electoral level there may even be some evidence – from recent British and French parliamentary elections – of European issues becoming more salient in both campaigning and voting behaviour.

Nonetheless, there are real structural constraints on the effective operation of the domestic accountability model (Lord, 1991). Philip Norton has argued that if national parliaments are to adapt to European integration they will themselves need to choose between an intergovernmental and a supranational approach – between individually constraining their own governments, or collectively checking the work of the Council. Yet, the first would be insufficient to overcome a fragmented pattern of accountability, and the second could well implode under the weight of institutional jealousies between national parliaments and the European Parliament. Instead of the two working in a seamless web of interparliamentary cooperation, the EP might come to regard national parliaments as making their own role redundant and national parliaments might reject coordination as a pretext for EP leadership (Norton, 1996: 185). Such, at any rate, was the lesson of the ill-fated assizes between national parliaments and the European Parliament, held in Rome in 1990.

Whatever the answer to this dilemma, accountability to national parliaments will probably always be inhibited by the non-transparency of Council decision making. Even though the draft Amsterdam Treaty will require the Council to legislate more openly, it will be very difficult to disinter deliberation from the labyrinthine complexes of committees that mingle Council activities with both national and Commission policy making (comitology), or to avoid all forms of 'soft-law' making that circumvent formal requirements of accountability to national parliaments. A Vice-President of the European Parliament has recently complained that greater scrutiny of the Council of Ministers has only shifted business towards the European Council, whose decisions executive-dominated national parliaments are less likely to criticise for fear of embarrassing heads of government. The conclusions of the European Council have multiplied from four pages to fifty and they now encroach on the two most important 'sectoral councils' of the Council of Ministers by incorporating the results of elaborate bargaining between Foreign and Finance Ministers (Institutional Affairs Committee of European Parliament, 22 September, 1997). As for 'soft-law' making, a typical example of this emerged with 'framework agreements' under the third pillar. These will intimately affect citizen rights without enjoying the status of formal law that has been scrutinised and ratified by due parliamentary process, and then placed on the public record. Factors such as these make it hard to establish formal political responsibility, to discover the reasons for decisions or even, sometimes, to ascertain what has been decided at all (Weidenfeld, 1994: 38). One consequence is that intergovernmental aspects of the Union's political system may offer considerable opportunity for 'blame shifting' or what has been described as the 'alibi-function', whereby governments use the European framework precisely because of the opportunities it offers to deny political responsibility and to disguise choices as constraints (Hill, 1983).

At base, the intergovernmental model assumes that preserving state sovereignty and domestic accountability amount to the same thing. In the context of European integration they do not. For, in their attempts to maintain their own sovereignty, state executives have attempted two democratically problematic strategies: first, they have supported a pattern of Euro-governance by permanent inter-state negotiation; and, second, they have accepted the effective abandonment of the unitary concept of the state, so that individual departments of national governments can mesh directly with the Commission, and do their best to penetrate its detailed policy making across the range of public administration. The former reminds us of Dahl's observation that diplomacy and democracy are incompatible modes of decision making. By applying foreign policy methods to Union activities constructed around a domestic agenda, governments have extended executive privilege to the core of democratic politics and subjected them to a bargaining format that requires secrecy rather than transparency. This has had the further effect of eroding the separation of power in national political systems as much as in the European: the power of national parliaments to check and balance their governments by denying them law-making authority is compromised by the power of executives to constitute themselves as legislatures in the Council of Ministers of the EU. As for the fusion of public administration at the two levels, Renaud Dehousse points out that political responsibility to national parliaments and electorates presupposes that governments should behave as unitary actors in the European arena and not shade off into a series of transnational policy communities (Richardson, 1996; Dehousse, 1997; Peterson, 1997).

Worse still, it has been impossible to apply the intergovernmental model in a 'pure form' that might have preserved its compatibility with domestic accountability. Compromises have had to be made with supranationalism for the sake of performance. Majority voting and the ECJ's energetic insistence on the supremacy of Union law have been accepted, and even supported, by governments: the latter because it has helped them make credibly binding commitments to one another, and the former because it has allowed the Council to sustain a central role in EU decision making, in spite of a widening membership and a growing agenda. But majority voting means that individual governments often cannot be held responsible for the decisions of the Council as a whole, and the supremacy of Union law means that even if a national electorate or parliament were to express a grievance through the removal of a national administration, the matter in question would remain binding law.

The overall lesson is that attempts to make one political system (the European) accountable through the institutions of another (the national) are unlikely to be satisfactory. Not only will they be dogged by information gaps between the two levels, the non-congruence of the two arenas will also cause insoluble logical difficulties such as the impossibility of any one parliament or electorate ever being in a position to remove the Union's political leadership as a whole. National parliaments are in a position to remove individual members of the Council. But, as we have seen, they cannot change the offending law itself, let alone the whole complex of Conciliar power relations. The European Parliament can remove the Commission (on a two-thirds vote). But, as we have also seen, that only constitutes a section of the Union's political leadership. As Joseph Weiler has put it, 'there is no real sense in which the European political process allows the electorate to throw the rascals out, or to take what is often the only ultimate power left to the people which is to replace one set of governors by another' (Weiler, 1997b: 275). This is a serious shortcoming, for one of the great strengths of liberal democratic systems is their ability to insulate the legitimacy of an institutional order from the effects of mistaken or unpopular policies by removing particular political leaderships. As a result, blame and failure can, in most liberal democracies, be attached to individuals or to particular governments, rather than the system itself. This is not so with the EU.

It follows from many of the things we have said, that the intergovernmental model may even lead to the *de*-democratisation of the state rather than the democratisation of the Union. Not only does it produce an adverse shift in the balance of power from parliaments to executives, as the latter are inherently better placed to organise at European level and, then, to use this as a political resource in domestic politics (Dehousse, 1997). It may also cause two contrasting forms of delegitimation in the electoral and party politics of member democracies. In some countries, attempts to hold the Union accountable through the domestic democratic process may encourage the rise of 'cartel parties', which seek to manage issues between themselves, rather than to compete freely for positions that meet with public approval (Katz and Mair, 1995): first, because the European integration issue often threatens the cohesion of party systems formed exclusively around domestic issues; second, because the resources of two political arenas – and not just one – can now be used to sustain any cartel of status quo parties; and, third, because Union bargaining will, in any case, involve governing parties in technicolour voting coalitions on the Council of Ministers, so complicating their scope to differentiate themselves domestically. On the other hand, there is also evidence of a contrary effect. Attempts by national democratic actors to hog the action at both levels may expose member democracies to new risks of destabilisation (Andeweg, 1995; Franklin, 1996). Where the same parties stand in European and national elections, the momentum of breakthroughs achieved in an electoral setting that is peculiarly propitious for protest parties can be sustained into normal national political competition. The classic example is the French National Front which benefited enormously from the 1984 European elections. But, 'anti-system' parties such as these can do considerable harm to the credibility of democratic politics. Because they soak up a significant proportion of the votes without being available for alignments with others, they can greatly restrict the scope for successful coalition building, limit the chances that a political system will produce both strong government and strong opposition, and increase the likelihood that majoritarian politics will produce perverse results.

The supranational model: can the EU develop a democracy of its own?

Given the problems of making the EU democratic through the representative institutions of its member states, an obvious answer might seem to be to endow it with a democracy of its own. The EU already has its own directly elected parliament, a system of trans-national party federations and parliamentary party groups (Hix and Lord, 1997) and an active set of political lobbies that provides possibilities for interest intermediation (Mazey and Richardson,

1993; Greenwood, 1997). These are, however, a mixture of the modest and the problematic. It is, accordingly, possible to imagine a variety of ways in which a supranational democracy might be more systematically constructed at the European level. A directly elected European Parliament could be given a final say in the making of new laws (on the assumption that the Council would also continue to enjoy such a power, this is known as legislative 'Co-decision'). It could also be given a fuller role in the formation and political survival of the Commission, analogous, perhaps, to arrangements in domestic politics where governments have to enjoy the confidence of a majority of elected representatives on a continuous basis. The Commission – or its Presidency – could even be directly elected by the citizenry of the Union as a whole (Bogdanor, 1986; Bogdanor, 1996), maybe with a system of US style primaries or a campaigning style in which contenders for office appear before national parliaments and their media (address by Irish Prime Minister, John Bruton, to conference of the European Peoples Party, European Parliament April 1995). And, finally, pan-Union referenda could be held on structural issues of European integration, possibly at the same time as elections to the European Parliament (Weiler, 1997b). Although these methods are very different, they raise common legitimation issues that can, once again, be analysed under our three-fold heading of authorisation, representation and accountability. Yet, more so than with the possibility of legitimating the Union through its component national democracies, we shall see that the difficulties of constructing a single democracy at the European level relate to a common theme: that of the absence of a European demos – the cluster of shared identities, meanings and communications that we considered in Chapter two.

Authorisation of power under the supranational model

An argument that is often made against a supranational democracy is that it would impart 'too much legitimacy' to the European Union. Although it is difficult to make much sense of the idea that holders of public office might have too much right to exercise their functions, the disquiet of those who argue in this way is poorly phrased, rather than misplaced. For, a problem with all the suggestions in the previous paragraph is that they would involve the Union in bidding for a kind of democratic legitimation that it might not easily achieve: that of authorisation by majoritarian democracy. In place of present arrangements that institutionalise a high level of power sharing across member states and party families, some countries and ideological tendencies would have to live for a long period of time with a Commission, parliamentary governing majority or referendum result for which they had not voted (Dehousse, 1995). In moments of extreme stress – or emotionally charged public debate – this could lead to splits in the Union, problematic forms of variable geometry or periods of non cooperation. There are probably four requirements of majoritarian method that are missing in the case of the EU.

- Normative agreement that this is the appropriate way to proceed.
- A high level of social homogeneity, so that even if a majority makes all the key decisions these are unlikely to be too far removed from the preferences of minorities (Lijphart, 1984: 22)
- A unidimensional structure of political preferences – if societies are cleaved in more than one way, a majority that is elected on one dimension will not necessarily correspond to majority opinion on others (Lijphart, 1984: 8). Representatives will tend to align differently on different issues. This will produce unstable executive authority where parliaments are responsible for government formation; and, even where they are limited to legislative functions, there will be indeterminacies, known as 'cycling': outcomes will be crucially shaped by what ought only to be an arbitrary and procedural consideration – the order in which issues are considered.
- A public opinion that is capable of being organised into recognisably coherent majorities, rather than chance agglomerations of the confused or inconsistent. The history of majoritarian systems would seem to suggest that the legitimacy of the majority is itself variable depending on how it scores in this regard.

Turning to a consideration of these factors in relation to the EU, Table 2.2 on page 54 suggests that public opinion in the Union is no better than evenly divided on whether a European majoritarianism would be normatively appropriate. The spread of preferences is obviously wider than in any one member state, several of which have already found it best to avoid majoritarian politics. In addition, the presence of the integration issue itself, and continued cultural-territorial segmentation, means that the Union is at least a three dimensional political system, with little prospect, therefore, of forming majorities that could stabilise across all elements of a governing programme. It faces, first, a substantive agenda of largely left-right issues; second, a constitutional debate on whether decisions are most appropriately taken by intergovernmental or supranational procedures; and, third, distributional conflict between member states or regions.

Nor does evidence from existing arrangements for supranational democracy in the Union encourage the view that public opinion would be easy to organise into coherent majorities at the European level. European elections have remained stubbornly 'second-order' since their inception in 1979. That is to say, voters rank the national arena as more important than the Europe, they use European elections to express preferences about domestic politics rather than the EU, and they turn out in lower numbers than for national elections. It is, therefore, difficult to interpret outcomes as a democratic authorisation of one approach to Union politics over another, or, indeed, as having anything much to do with the EU at all (Reif and Schmitt, 1980; Franklin in Richardson, 1996: 187). Now, it is, of course, possible that a decision to strengthen Union-level democracy could of itself remove the second-order problem. If, for example, the European Parliament had the power to determine the political leadership of the Union, voters might be far more inclined to turn out and to vote along European lines. We should not, however, bank on this. Voter participation has fallen in all of the four elections since 1979, even though the EP has gained more power, including, in 1994, the new right to confirm the Commission in office. There would seem to be at least two difficulties. The second-order pattern has powerfully self-reinforcing characteristics. So long as voters and other political parties play the second-order game, it is very risky for any one national party leadership not to follow suit. Yet each European election fought in this way perpetuates national patterns of electoral choice by forfeiting opportunities for what David Held calls developmental democracy: the process by which any political system can become progressively more democratic as voting and other forms of participation spread understanding of institutional frameworks, and skill the public in the effective use of representative structures (Held, 1996: 115–18). In any case, the second-order pattern goes deeper than the assignment of political powers to this or that level of democratic competition. It has to do with cultural features that limit the formation of a

European demos. In other words, with the problems reviewed in the last chapter.

Representation under the supranational model

As shown in cell 5 of Table 3.1, representation under the supranational model would consist in some combination of a political leadership elected at Union level, together with a European parliament organised into transnational ideological groupings, rather than national delegations. Given that the idea of representative democracy is that the public should rule without having to assume the burden of collective decision, the goal of any system of representation is to put the few who do hold power under systematic pressure to anticipate the needs and values of the many. For this link to work, the following conditions would ideally exist.

- The insertion of the public's representatives into strategic positions in the political system where they are able to confer or withhold power, or deny resources, such as finance and legislative authority, that are needed for the effective exercise of power.
- Incentives for representatives to link society to governance by searching out and articulating the principal issue cleavages that define the interests of social groups in relation to the political system.
- An opportunity for the public to choose between 'rival partisan programmes' at the 'same level of aggregation' as the political system itself (Schmitter, 1996).

Only a supranational system of representation – in which voters, parties and a Parliament come together at the European level – would seem to be capable of satisfying the second and third of these conditions. It would also seem fairly straightforward for such a system to satisfy the first condition. For even though it might be felt too majoritarian for it to have powers of government formation, the EP could be allowed to develop as a strong representative body along the lines of the US Congress, whose very considerable hold over executive office holders derives from powers over finance and law-making. Free of pressures to organise a governing majority, such a European Parliament could even be less susceptible to executive domination than many national parliaments in Europe and freer, therefore, to concentrate on being a public forum, debating, not least of all, questions of how the Union's political system might be developed (Attinà, 1990). Moreover, majoritarianism in the making of laws and the passing of budgets is very different, and more appropriate to the European Union, than majoritarianism in the formation of governments. As legislative majorities can afford to be fluid while governing majorities need to be stable, a European Parliament that concentrated on representing the public through its powers over finance and law-making, rather than through the making and breaking of governments, would have far more scope to arrange a distributive, or inclusive pattern of benefits, in which those who lose on some issues win on others. This is, to reiterate, a sensible arrangement where a political system is characterised by multiple and cross-cutting cleavages, and where a sense of political identity is underdeveloped.

Unlike domestic parliamentarians, MEPs are in a position to specialise in the full-time task of following the EU and influencing its decision-making. They have a permanent presence in the EU's political system and ready access to those who hold executive power, with both the Commission and Council attending all plenaries and committees of the Parliament. On the other hand, 'representation at the level of the political system itself' is inherently problematic when the entity in question is a transnational and multilingual union of 370 million people stretched out from Lisbon to Helsinki. MEPs may become detached from public opinion. A somewhat light-hearted view of how all this can lead to an introverted concern with the internal affairs of the Parliament, rather than effective representation of outside society, is provided by Marc Abelès' anthropological study of the EP: 'MEPs are a long way from their country of origin . . . it is often difficult for them to comprehend the tasks they are expected to perform . . . deterritorialised the MEP searches for new solidarities . . . without a doubt the party group plays the role of a cacoon' (Abelès, 1992: 148–155).

However, present arrangements suggest the possibility of an even more fundamental weakness in supranational democracy: the second order character of European elections breaks the circuit in the politics of representation by removing systemic pressure on MEPs to cooperate and compete in a manner that anticipates public opinion. For, the political fate of MEPs is not connected to anything they themselves do, but to factors beyond their direct control, such as the relationship between the national and European electoral cycles and the mid-term unpopularity of governments (Attinà, 1998). In conditions in which the electoral process is arbitrarily related to the performance of MEPs, and (re)selection of candidates tends to be centralised in national party bureaucracies, it is national parties – rather than a European wide electorate – that have the real power to reward and sanction the careers of MEPs. This means that the EP is not as free from executive domination – by members of the Council and European Council – as appears at first sight. There is, for example, powerful evidence that MEPs from national parties of government came under intense pressure during the vote of Parliamentary confirmation on the Presidency of Jacques Santer, so limiting the independence with which the EP could exercise an important new power and, effectively, collapsing the supranational principle of representation back into a further application of the intergovernmental one (Hix and Lord, 1996: 64).

National parties likewise dominate the framing of programmes for Euro-elections via the party federations of the Union, and, in any case, these manifestos struggle to find recognition in the campaigns themselves. This, once again, limits the emergence of cleavages and choices at the level of the political system itself. To the extent that MEPs are elected under national party labels but form themselves into transnational groupings once they arrive at the European Parliament, all would not seem to be lost. For such a situation could even be defended as reconciling effective supranational representation with continued citizen choice between familiar national parties, so long as the transnational party families broadly correspond to the ideological streams to be found at national level and MEPs stay true to the alignments under which they were elected. The difficulty is that neither of these conditions apply. Alignments in the European Parliament depart quite markedly from those in national electoral arenas and more seats change hands between elections than as a direct result of voter choice (Andeweg, 1995: 61; Bardi, 1994: 365).

So, to summarise, the problems we have reviewed – the lack of a Euro-electorate, of a properly integrated party system and of full parliamentary powers – all interact with one another to form a self-reinforcing set of constraints that keeps supranational representative politics in the EU in a kind of sub-optimal equilibrium. It is hard to see how any one set of actors can break out of constraints on the creation of a Euro-democracy without all the others doing so.

Accountability under the supranational model

Cell 6 of Table 3.1 shows that accountability under the supra-national model would consist in the need for the executive power of the Union – the Council and the Commission – to be politically responsible to a powerful European Parliament, which would, in turn, be answerable to a Europe-wide electorate. Some argue that accountability is the most important of our three components of democratic legitimation. Such are the indeterminacies of aggregating preferences – and the undesirability of even attempting to do this on all issues and at all moments – that the anticipation of public opinion is a hopeless task; and, in any case, governing elites are often regarded as being elected to use their own judgement, subject to the sanction that if they get things wrong they can always be brought to account after the event (Schumpeter, 1943; Plamenatz, 1973: 118). Accountability may, in turn, take many forms, amongst which the following are the most obvious: the need for office holders to give reasons for decisions, to defend them, and answer questions before the public or its representatives; exposure to judicial review by the courts; and, of course, removal from office, either by failure at the ballot box, or by censure by an elected assembly. The appropriate method of accountability is to a certain extent linked to the nature of the task. The exercise of powers which require the impartial weighing of individual rights is best brought to account by judicial review, for majoritarian assemblies or elections may only compound the oppression of the individual (Majone, 1996: 285). Conversely, the latter are best suited to questions that involve a diffuse collective interest, including the broad definition of the overall framework of individual rights within which judicial review operates.

A system of effective supranational accountability would probably require some mix of four linked components. First, transparency of process, so that the public, its representatives at the European level and the courts could view, understand, and receive justifications, for executive decisions. Second, obligations on the Union's leadership to give explanations and answer questions to a publicly visible European Parliament, which would need, in turn, to be endowed with sanctions that might vary from the power to embarrass to the removal of office holders. Third, a strong and accessible European Court of Justice. Fourth, scope for the public to use Euro-elections to remove the Union's political leadership or to 'guard the guardians' by sanctioning members of a European Parliament who have been insufficiently vigilant on their behalf. Now the Union as presently constituted has a mixed score card on these criteria. In spite of very few sanctions, the European Court of Justice has been remarkably effective in bringing both Union institutions and national governments to account for their treatment of individuals under Union law, often enforcing standards that do not exist in particular member countries. We will examine some of the possible reasons for this in the next chapter. The European Parliament is, as we have seen, freer than its national counterparts of executive domination, and this may increase its freedom to criticise without fear or favour. On the other hand, we have also seen that the second-order pattern of European elections breaks the link of political responsibility between voter choice and the behaviour of European office holders, whether executive or parliamentary; and that any EP independence may be conditional upon a pattern of European parliamentary accountability that is relatively costless to the member states.

Above all, the EP's problems in the area of accountability are the mirror image of those of national parliaments and electorates. In a context where European and national authorities are often administratively fused and jointly responsible for errors, the only feasible solution may be to proceed against the whole of the Union's political leadership, until all involved in Council and Commission decision making suspend the game of blame shifting and offer up credible answers as to precisely who was responsible for incompetence or wrongdoing. But the EP can no more remove national governments from office than domestic actors can sanction Union institutions. The constraints that such discontinuities place on democratic accountability were perfectly illustrated by the EP's special committee of enquiry into the beef crisis (Medina Ortega report, European Parliament, 1997). As the spokesperson for the European People's Party put it in the plenary debate: 'Primary responsibility lies with the British Government, and secondary responsibility with an earlier Commission. The Commission can only be as good in any case as each member state lets it be' (Reimer Böge MEP, European Parliament, Verbatim Report of Proceedings, 18 February, 1997). Yet the Parliament's powers of sanction were confined to the lesser culprit, and most, absurdly of all, to a Commission that had not even been in office at the time when any mistakes were made. In contrast, the British minister, whose government had been in power in the 1980s, could not even be compelled to attend the enquiry.

A further structural problem is presented by our earlier observation that the transnational character of the Euro-polity requires extreme consensus democracy. This, in turn, means that executive office has to be carefully distributed across member states and mainstream partisan perspectives. So, even if the Parliament or electorate were given more powers to form or remove the Union's political leadership, any replacement would probably have to be constructed along much the same lines. On the other hand, domestic electorates could, of course, make more coordinated assaults on members of the Council, in response to European parliamentary criticisms, but that returns us to the lack of demos, or relatively underdeveloped political communications at the popular level.

Interactions between democratic legitimacy at the national and Union levels

It is evident from what we have said so far, that the Union has created mutually complicating relationships between democratic legitimation at the national and European levels, and this, in many ways, is what has confounded both of the most obvious routes to its democratisation. The difficulty with the intergovernmental approach is that domestic institutions may be *de*-democratised, rather than the EU legitimated, by attempts to link the two arenas. The problem with the supranational approach is that it will not be enough to replicate the mechanics of representative democracy at the European level where publics and elites continue to care more about competition for power in domestic politics, or where they are otherwise culturally constrained from forming a Euro-demos. To put either intergovernmental or supranational solutions on a sounder footing would, for different reasons, require a sharper differentiation between the national and European arenas: clearer lines of political responsibility – including less majority voting and less administrative fusion – would be needed for the Union to be democratised through domestic institutions; more opportunities to decouple the competition for power in European institutions from that in national politics, would be needed for a supranational Euro-democracy to work. The difficulty with all of this, however, is that there are very good reasons from the point of view of our other two dimensions of legitimacy – identity and performance – for believing that there should be a high level of fusion between the European and national levels at this point in the Union's political development.

So, must we conclude that the only satisfactory solution from a point of view of democratic legitimation is to give up on European integration, intergovernmental or supranational, and return to a situation in which politics are confined to the nation state? Surely not. For, in contemporary conditions, mutually complicating interactions, from a point of view of democracy, would exist between the transnational and national levels, with or without Union institutions (Held, 1996; Touraine, 1994). As Fritz Scharpf has put it, the criticism that it is going to be more difficult to organise responsive government at the European than the national level relates only to the *input* side of democracy, the problems that arise from feeding popular needs and values into a machine that is more remote and aggregated than the state. As far as the *output* side is concerned, the Union may have far more capacity than free-standing states to show responsiveness to certain kinds of public need (Scharpf, 1997: 19). What these might be we will consider in the next chapter. So, whatever happens, there may be awkward choices to be made between national democracies with well developed democratic identities but restricted capacity to meet some kinds of public need, and European democracy, with its underdeveloped demos but greater scope to tackle important collective action problems, whose resolution is close to what many of us mean when we talk about a democratically self-governing society.

Within any decision to allocate political values through European institutions, a further choice will then have to be made between intergovernmental and supranational approaches to democratisation, neither of which are likely to offer ideal answers at this stage in the Union's development. And solutions will be all the more radically contested to the extent that values and circumstances differ across individual member societies. The most obvious difficulty here is that each national political system has tended to embed various – and not always compatible – ideas of what constitutes legitimate democratic practice in its citizenry. Likewise the democratic machinery of each member country is affected in its own peculiar way by the operation of the European Union (Schmidt, 1997: 129). The following are amongst the most important of the differences between national societies that may make it difficult to design one European structure that can satisfy the democratic expectations of all.

I Differences in the quality of domestic democratic practice

People from countries where democracy has performed well (Scandinavian countries) are more likely to regard consociational approaches as the most appropriate at Union level, because they are reluctant to lose the benefit of their own domestic institutions. In contrast, a supranational democracy may be regarded as a welcome substitute for national institutions that have failed to produce good governance (Italy). In these cases, consociational approaches at Union level will not be very attractive because they only yield a democracy that is as good as arrangements for representation in the national 'segments' of the Union; indeed, inter-governmental patterns of representation in the EU may tend to entrench the role of established domestic elites. Table 2.2 on page 54 illustrates this contrast very clearly. Even amongst elite opinion, support for a European Parliament with full co-decision with the Council is remarkably low in Denmark and Sweden, compared with, say, Italy.

2 Differences in what is regarded as appropriate executive discretion

This is relevant to the legitimacy of EU decisions in two ways: first, because the Union contains independent branches of government, such as the European Commission and (eventually) the European Central Bank; and, second, because the whole logic of the Community method is, as we have seen, to loosen domestic constraints on national executive authority. Amongst member states, there are some interesting contrasts that help explain the differential acceptability of these two features of the Union's political system. In Germany, for example, the legitimacy of the Commission is largely accepted; and a Monetary Union would be regarded as less, rather than more, legitimate if it were not entrusted to an independent Central Bank. On the other hand, the tendency of Council politics to increase the discretionary powers of the German Federal Government has been a cause of some anxiety, for it is potentially subversive of the checks and balances, and multi-level pattern of governance, that have been so important to legitimating national executive authority in postwar Germany. In contrast, things have tended to be the other way round in France: the establishment of the European Council was regarded in the mid-1970s as enhancing the legitimacy of the Union because it meant that major decisions had to be approved by the French Presidency, which is democratically elected by the entire French nation. The Commission, however, is still regarded in some quarters as only a technical body with no right to a political role. And the notion of an independent Central Bank is usually only accepted with the caveat that it should be accompanied by a more political – and democratic – layer of European economic governance.

3 Whether national democracies have been institutionalised through majoritarian or consensus practices

As we shall see, the EU, is for good reasons, an extreme form of consensus democracy. This means that it tries to align itself with the preferences of the greatest number, rather than those of the majority (Lijphart, 1984). It emphasises collegiate modes of decision making; it always includes a wide range of party political influences; and it practices 'cooperative federalism' (where member states and centre share control for each issue area, rather than attempt to divide jurisdictions in a way that reduces necessary contact between the levels). Now there are political systems in Western Europe – notably Germany and the Benelux countries – where all of this is just an extension of normal democratic practice. There are others, such as the UK, where contestation and government by a directly elected majority is often considered the only form of democracy, with the result that the existing democratic qualities of the Union are often not appreciated, and the prospect that the EU might develop into a fully-fledged democracy strikes a note of fear amongst those who, wrongly, believe that this can only lead to a coercive from of European level majoritarianism. Table 3.2 provides one estimated ranking of EU countries on a consensus-majoritarian dimension.

4 Extent to which democracy is bound up with nationhood

In some member states the values of democracy and nationhood are regarded as standing in a self-reinforcing relationship: democracy is seen as the 'self-governing nation in action'; and only nationhood is thought capable of yielding the solidarity needed for

Table 3.2 Where member states stand on a scale of consensus and majoritarian democracy

EU member country	Score on consensus-majoritarian dimension
Belgium	4.22
Finland	3.71
Italy	3.70
Denmark	1.10
The Netherlands	0.99
Sweden	−0.29
France	−0.50
Germany	−0.64
Austria	−2.64
Ireland	−3.55
Luxembourg	−4.28
UK	−10.41

Source: Mair (1994: 120)

democracy to function. Ideas such as these obviously limit the transferability of democracy from national to transnational levels: a European democracy is either seen as implausible, or, in the unlikely even of it working, as destructive of nationhood. Other political cultures, however, are far more likely to regard democracy as a movable feast that can be constructed within any group whose members are prepared to regard its decisions as binding. Among EU countries where democracy and nationhood are thought to be intimately connected are: Britain, France and Scandinavia.

5 Degree of congruence between 'winning solutions' under national and EU democratic institutions

It is a fair surmise that EU decisions will be easier to accept the closer they are to the outcomes that would have emerged from national democratic institutions in the absence of any European Union. Geoffrey Garrett and George Tsibilis demonstrate that even governments that have the same voting weights on the Council of Ministers will vary in what they get out of the process, depending on how close they are to the centre of the different dimensions along which political values are arrayed in Union politics. Those dimensions may be intergovernmentalism versus supranationalism, left versus right, or north versus south. A government that occupies a mid-point along several dimensions is likely to be very satisfied with the outcomes of Union decision making, not least because the Union's decision rules require over-sized coalitions that have to include 'centre positions'. A government that is an 'outlier' (occupies an extreme point) on several dimensions is likely to be dissatisfied. To the extent that informal majority voting tends to anticipate the decision rules, these findings may hold even where voting is infrequent (Garrett and Tsibilis, 1996).

6 Whether democratisation of national arenas preceded European integration or was in some ways dependent upon it

In several EU countries, democratisation was facilitated or consolidated by European integration. The need for the Southern European countries to democratise to attain membership of the Union provides one obvious example. However, even amongst the original Six, and in Germany in particular, the original European Community was seen as reducing international securities that had fanned pathological and non-democratic politics before 1945. In countries such as these, European integration may find legitimacy as an external guarantor of democracy, rather than as a source of democratic governance in its own right. In other Union countries, however, democracy was secured well before the formation of the Union (Britain and the Scandanavian countries) and the dependence of the one on the other is less apparent.

7 Extent to which parameters of choice in domestic arenas are affected by European integration

Many national democracies may be tightly constrained by a series of external factors: size, resources and globalisation being the most important. In political systems such as these, European integration can even be seen as enlargening the scope of democratic public choice, with positive results for the legitimacy of collective decision at the European level. An interesting case study is provided by the history of the European centre left in recent years. When, in 1979, the transnational Party of European Socialists (PES) attempted to launch a common manifesto at a press conference, the British Prime Minister was more interested in using the occasion to protest the independence of the Labour Party. Then, in the ensuing years, two of the main centre-left parties in Western Europe lost power (British Labour and German SPD) and two more found that even those who won control of the domestic arena had to scale down their ambitions (French and Spanish Socialists). From the end of the 1980s, there was clear evidence of growing willingness on the European centre left to accept the legitimacy of collaborative action. Indications of this included the growing cohesion in the PES group in the European Parliament; the institution of summits between leaders of parties belonging to the PES; and a new constitution that allowed for majority voting between national parties that belonged to the Federation (Hix and Lord, forthcoming).

8 Pattern of national elite support for democratisation process at EU level

French political elites have, for example, given little support to developing the legitimacy of the European Parliament, with the result that the quality of representation offered by French MEPs has been sharply criticised. The French delegation suffers from high absenteeism and turnover between parliaments and many of its members hold double or even treble mandates (together with seats in the National Assembly or positions as local mayors). One author has described them as regarding the European Parliament as a mixture between a nursery school (for those beginning their careers), a convalescence ward (for the temporarily wounded) and a retirement home (for those ending their careers) (Andolfato, 1994). In contrast, French governments of both parties have done a great deal to promote the idea that the EU can be adequately democratised and legitimated through the Council.

Conclusion and implications for the shape of the EU political system

To recapitulate, we have argued that there are deep-seated problems with either route by which the EU might be democratised: whether intergovernmental or supranational methods are employed, authorisation, representation and accountability are inherently difficult to institutionalise at the European level. The resulting legitimation deficit has important implications for the character of power relations in the EU and for the shape of its political system. It is to this theme that we now turn by way of conclusion.

Now, one obvious solution for political systems where there is room for disagreement about legitimating criteria is to embed elements of more than one approach in the structure of power relations. Many of the states that make up the EU provide historical examples. For much of the eighteenth and nineteenth centuries, legitimate government in Britain required a mixture of electoral authorisation (albeit on a limited and sometimes corrupt franchise) and royal approval. The French Third Republic (1871–1940) was constructed on the legitimating principles of the French revolution. But it was also strongly representative of conservative interests (Thomson, 1969: 101). We have likewise seen during the course of this chapter that the EU practises dual legitimation across the range of its institutional structures. Important examples include the split political leadership in which a supranational body (Commission) proposes and an intergovernmental one (Council) decides: the pervasive practice of *Politikverflechtung* whereby the European and national levels of government make no attempt to remain rigidly separate jurisdictions but try, instead, to fuse their activities across the range of policy-making; acknowledgement that both national parliaments and a supranational parliament have roles to play in providing consent, representation and accountability; and arrangements whereby the Commission is appointed by member states but confirmed in office by the EP.

We have seen that there are, indeed, good reasons for the EU to practise dual legitimation. A political system, like the EU, that is in the process of formation may aspire to the construction of some new form of legitimacy, but it must, in the meantime, work with established notions of what constitutes rightful political authority. In the case of the EU, there is the further problem that the relative legitimacy of intergovernmental and supranational approaches to EU democratisation varies across the sub-units of the Union; and, moreover, the Union has not yet completed the process of adding further societies, which will often, for the first years of their membership, be characterised by low political socialisation into the EU's normative order. Finally, there is the pervasive tension which underlines Union politics: on the one hand, patterns of identity point to a continued need for cultural-territorial methods of representation; on the other, the EU has a substantive agenda that provokes a pattern of choices and conflicts that cross-cut national divisions, so calling for an element of debate and coalition formation at European level.

Dual legitimation, however, brings problems of its own. Almost all political systems that adopt approaches such as these suffer from moments of crisis and stress. When decisions that are allocative of fundamental political values can no longer be avoided, the legitimacy of the mixed system is usually questioned by those who feel that they would do better under just one of the approaches to the legitimation of power. In fact, dual legitimation often works best in conservative political contexts, because the most obvious way of combining two legitimating principles is to give a mutual veto to those who embody each approach. This carries an obvious risk of immobilise and frustration with the overall structure of power relations.

One consequence of its need to seek dual (supranational/intergovernmental) legitimation is that the democratic politics that are practised in the Union take the form of an extreme consensus democracy with the following features:

- The need for unanimous consent of member states for many 'constitutional' changes and basic decisions of policy assignment. This contrasts with systems where a two-thirds majority is sufficient.
- Supervision of the Union's agenda by a body – the European Council – that can usually only reach agreement by unanimous consent of the member governments. (One of the few exceptions to this is the calling of Intergovernmental Conferences.)
- The use of over-sized majorities on detailed questions of policy formulation and implementation. These work out at 71 per cent of the weighted votes on the Council and, in practice, at much the same level in the European Parliament (where a measure can only be passed on an absolute majority of the membership, not just of those voting on the day).
- The need for a high level of agreement across the range of EU institutions (Commission, Council and, increasingly, the European Parliament), each of which is appointed on a different basis.
- The need for high levels of collaboration across the levels of government – national and European – to get anything done.
- The need to achieve the consent of non-state actors who are the direct addressees of Union policy and whose cooperation is needed in specialist areas of policy making.
- A growing need to respond to strands of public opinion that cannot be aggregated through the 'club of governments', either

because their full force can only be felt transnationally or because they represent minorities within member states. The EP offers some help here, though, as we have repeatedly seen, not enough.

On the other hand, this elaborate search for consensus has produced pathologies of its own. In tackling one set of legitimation problems – the need to get the broadest possible consent – the Union has tended to create another raft of difficulties: the non-transparency and incomprehensibility of its decision making; a cartelisation of politics by governments and other established interests; a measure of private (rather than public) interest governance; a reduction in political contestation; and a sense that the 'scoundrels cannot be thrown out' because it will always be necessary to engage the same elite combinations in Union governance. To the extent that these problems derive, in turn, from constraints on the acceptability of majoritarianism at Union level, the problems of identity formation, which we reviewed in the last chapter, carry over into the democratisation of the Union. Many commentators have hoped that legitimation by superior governing performance, the topic of the next chapter, might compensate the Union for weaknesses of democratic legitimacy and identity formation. If this is to happen, however, the Union may need to provide substantial 'value added', either directly or by strengthening the capacity of member states to meet public needs. For the problems of identity and democracy are not only grave in themselves; they also have a potential to inhibit performance which must, accordingly, yield very high returns if it is to cover the high overhead of mediating problems through the EU's political system. It is to the issue of legitimation through performance that we now turn.

CHAPTER FOUR

Performance

Introduction

The European Union has acquired a substantial portfolio of policies. It covers almost as many areas of public concern as its member states. It distributes resources between countries, and it allocates values between individuals in a manner that affects their life chances. Political powers that impose sacrifices on some and open opportunities to others are in need of justification (Beetham, 1991). Yet we have seen that the Union is problematic both as a democracy and as a collective identity. Might it, however, justify its powers on the utilitarian grounds that certain fundamental needs and values can only be met by a European structure of governance? If so, what needs and values? And whose? Would all institutional responses be equally legitimate? And what might be the implications of all of this for the character of power relations at the European and national levels? It is questions such as these that we address in this chapter.

The possibility of utilitarian justification has always been central to the analysis and practice of European integration. Jean Monnet once argued that the European Community would operate as a 'public utility state' (Meehan, 1993: 45) and academic perspectives have, likewise, tended to privilege performance over our two other criteria of legitimation, identity and democracy. Intergovernmentalists argue that the Union cannot and ought not to be a democracy and identity, but its powers are defensible to the extent that they contribute to the effective functioning of national political systems that are both of those things. In their view, the legitimating consequences of European integration are, paradoxically, limited to improving the performance of the state, and governments have enormous power to prevent the Union doing more than that.

In contrast, neofunctionalists believe that it is the Union itself that will be cumulatively legitimated by a record of superior performance. But, to the extent they predict that democratisation and identity formation will 'spill-over' from effective governance at the European level, they too imply that the Union will, for a certain period of its development, have to draw its legitimation almost exclusively from its capacity to meet basic needs that cannot be adequately delivered by the state acting alone.

Many claims and counterclaims are made about the relative effectiveness of policies made at the Union and national levels. But can we identify a set of general conditions under which one level of government – say, the EU – is systematically more likely to produce better governing performance than another, such as the nation state? Public choice theory attempts to do just that. Social scientists in that tradition believe that what makes public choice justifiable is the likelihood that private actions will fail (Olson, 1965). Prominent market failures are *negative externalities,* where individuals do not pay the full price of harms they create; and *public goods,* where they do not receive the full benefit of some good they do. So, for example, in the absence of government you might expect an excess of pollution (externality) and an under-provision of environmental services (public good). Once, however, countries pass a certain threshold of interdependence, the state may cease to be a viable corrective and become more of a problem than a solution: as Iain Begg and Nigel Grimwade put it, the 'domain' of public policy-making may be wider than the state and 'policy choices in one jurisdiction may have significant effects in another' (Begg and Grimwade in Edwards and Pijpers, 1997). It may, therefore, be in the interests of national governments to aid and abet their own producers in the displacement of costs to other countries, or to free ride on the efforts of neighbours to provide public goods. Under such conditions, the state may lose its legitimacy as a means of controlling for the harmful effects of private actions; unless, that is, it is complemented by transnational institutions.

Now, a whole raft of EU policies clearly can be justified as responses to market failures that spill across national political boundaries or as efforts to provide international public goods. Compelling examples are provided by policies which relate to the

physical environment, where West Europe has significant concentrations of population, shared seas, a linked river system and
prevailing winds that blow pollution towards countries on the north
and eastern sides of the Union (Wallace, 1990). Fish, for instance,
are what public choice theorists call a 'common pool resource':
they can be freely appropriated by those who do not pay for their
replacement and then sold as private goods (Ostrom and Walker,
1997: 40). Without public controls, there would be a 'race to fish
the last fish out of the sea'. Where, however, the breeding patterns
of fish do not respect national boundaries, or historical rights
allow different nationals to fish in each others' waters, states may
aggravate, rather than solve problems of over-exploitation. They
may align with their own fishing interests to encourage excessive
catches for fear that, if they do not act in such a way, others will.

The Single Market may also call for a transfer of important
state responsibilities for the correction of market failure to the EU.
In a single market, a supranational competition policy is justifiable,
first, because governments might not restrain their companies
from abusing market power where monopoly rents accrue in other
jurisdictions (Gatsios and Seabright, 1989) and, second, because
they might otherwise compete to subsidise their industries, so
misallocating resources and producing over-capacity. Conversely,
the Union's framework programme for the promotion of techno-
logical diffusion has been justified on the basis that corporate
earnings in some sectors are attributable to 'positive externalities':
the benefits of producers learning from one another. While this
may make it logical for public policy to promote networking and
clustering of high-tech companies, national authorities will only
have the authority, and incentive, to do this in their own jurisdictions, rather than across the Single Market as a whole. Likewise,
the costs of macroeconomic mismanagement may not be fully
internalised to the offending country. A soft currency policy (in so
far as this remains possible) may amount to a unilateral attempt
by one country to claim a trading preference for its own producers,
thereby re-fragmenting the single market.

These public choice arguments have some validity, in two respects. First, because they correspond to statements that the Union
has itself made to justify its own powers. The main principle of
policy assignment in the EU is the doctrine of subsidiarity, defined
in the Treaty of European Union as follows: the Union should
only act where it is better placed than national governments to do

so for reasons of scale or effects (Article 3b). This clearly covers the provision of public goods and the management of cross-border problems. Second, an important criterion for legitimating any structure of government on the basis of performance is that all members of society should, in principle, be capable of benefiting (Beetham, 1991). The idea that political bodies should be constructed to correct market failures fulfills this criterion very neatly. For where such failures exist, it should always be possible to eliminate them, to compensate all those who have had to change their ways and *still* enjoy some social return on the more efficient use of resources. In the technical jargon, EU institutions can be justified as helping those who live in its member states to move towards a 'pareto frontier' – a point of maximum efficiency at which no one can be made better off without making someone else worth off. Payments under the social funds to aid the restructuring of communities whose primary source of employment has disappeared as a result of market integration – and transfers under the structural funds to member states whose infrastructure is less adapted to international competition – both provide instances of Union frameworks being used as compensationary mechanisms to generalise the benefits of collective action.

Now, it clearly would be difficult to see any need for the EU if there were no shared collective action problems, such as harms that spill across national boundaries or international public goods that go under-provided. That said, public choice, at best, only produces a 'first take' on the value of institutions and, at worst, seriously misrepresents the manner in which performance contributes to the legitimation of political power. It is, moreover, important to get this straight if we are to arrive at a satisfactory account of what would count as a utilitarian justification for the European Union. Without wishing to get into complex methodological debates, let us take the following as the central claim that public choice theorists make about the analysis of legitimacy. We are, they believe, all motivated by *personal* preferences and interests that can be used as external – or objective – tests of institutions precisely because they are formed independently of those processes or, indeed, of any dialogue between individuals. Now let us turn this up-side down with four assumptions that are surely much more plausible: first, that actors – especially those in the public sphere – are motivated by *shared* values and 'rules of appropriateness' (Beetham, 1991); second, that they are heavily influenced by political *debate* and *discourse*; third, that they are guided in political matters by *socially constructed* simplifications of how cause relates to effect, for this is the only way of coping with the overwhelming complexity and uncertainty of mass society (Kahnemann *et al.*, 1982); and, fourth, that it follows from what we have just said about the bounded rationality of actors (Steinbruner, 1974; Simon, 1983) and the essentially ethical character of politics, that there are no 'efficiency solutions' in the use of information, resources and institutional technologies – there are only justifiable ones. As we proceed, we will see that various things follow from all of this, not least the need to give up on any pretension to define tests of legitimacy from outside the political or public sphere itself. For the moment, however, our concern is to point out that legitimation by performance will be best conceived as the delivery of socially defined rights or entitlements. For, to attempt to dig down further to individual preferences and interests is too reductionist in the sense that these things are themselves conditioned by shared norms. As Plamenatz once put it:

> the wants of people cannot be defined apart from the rights and duties, and the forms of social intercourse, supposed to be the means of achieving them ... Wants are both less stable and less definite than rights or duties. It is much more difficult to decide whether or not wants are satisfied than it is to decide whether or not rights are secure.   (Plamenatz, 1973: 182)

Now, what kind of rights delivery might justify the assignment of political powers to the European Union? We suggest that it is useful to answer this question under three heads: the right of the citizen to physical security, to economic and welfare entitlements, and to civic-legal liberties.

Legitimation by performance: three kinds of rights delivery

Security rights delivery

A primary justification for the European state was that it was the mechanism most likely to provide security with minimum harm to those it was supposed to protect. Externally, states would produce the best imaginable trade-off between the autonomy of national communities and international order, for, even in the absence of an over-arching international organisation, they would deter aggressors by operating a balance of power system. Internally, they would develop a monopoly of violence that would be safer than allowing 'protective agencies' to compete with one another, or, in plain English, letting people take the law into their own hands (Locke, 1952; Nozick, 1974: 120).

Although the EU is only tangentially a security provider, its legitimation proceeds, in significant part, from a break down in the foregoing case for organising security around states that are externally autonomous and internally monopolistic. The idea that each state could 'help itself' to security without the aid of common institutions (Waltz, 1979) eventually proved self defeating in the European region. Whereas it may have been possible in the eighteenth and nineteenth centuries to run a competitive states system without too much collateral damage to national societies (Jane Austen would write six novels almost without mention of the Napoleonic wars), European countries later responded to the logic of balance of power competition by progressively cranking up the level of social mobilisation in the event of hostilities. By the time of the 1939–45 war, historians would argue that boundaries between direct military combatants and civilian society had disappeared: conflict now took the form of 'total war' of unlimited liability to the very societies that states were supposed to protect (Calvocoressi and Wint, 1972). Moreover, a contradiction developed between the stability of states within the system and the stability of the system itself (Jervis, 1976: 78–82; Buzan, 1991: 294–319): the outbreak of the First World War showed how individual states could come under enormous pressure to behave in collectively irrational ways. This became especially dangerous when developments between 1870 and 1945 made it doubtful whether there was any inherent equilibrium – or balance of power – in the European area: if Germany were united, it would be in a position to dominate weaker neighbours; if, on the other hand, it were to be denied the right to national unity or subjected to restrictions that did not apply to other states, it would be prone to aggressive and *ravanchiste* politics (Gruner, 1989). The period of 1914–45 has, therefore, been plausibly represented as a single cycle of violence (Carr, 1964) that could only be terminated by finding a new organising principle for European politics. The degeneration of international politics in the region interacted with the considerable abuse of citizens by their own states. This, in turn, made it difficult to believe that unconstrained state monopolies of violence really were the best way of protecting people against internal security threats.

Against a background in which an unconstrained state system came to be seen as more of a menace than a protection to its citizens, European integration has often been justified to the public as a means of terminating conflict. In what is generally taken to have been the founding moment of the European Community – Robert Schuman's press conference of 9 May, 1950 – the French Foreign Minister argued that the Second World War had only come about because 'Europe had not been made' earlier; in contrast, war would be 'not only unthinkable but materially impossible' if France and Germany merged their coal and steel industries (Bullen and Pelly, 1986: 2). When the Treaty of Paris was signed a year later, its preamble justified the new Community as a means of terminating 'age-old rivalries' and 'creating the basis of a broader and deeper community among people long divided by bloody conflicts' (European Communities, 1987). Even in the contemporary era, Monetary Union is often justified as a means of locking European countries into a consensual state system. German reunification and the end of the cold war, it is frequently argued, necessitated an intensification of integration to counteract Germany's new capacity to develop its power unilaterally. Meanwhile, the pooling of coal and steel – key industries of the 1950s – had ceased to make uncooperative behaviour 'materially impossible'. A single currency would provide a new way of binding states into the Union and of committing them to its effective functioning. Imagine what might be involved in attempting to bail out of integration by resubstituting national currencies for a European one: under modern conditions, the minimum replacement period of one form of money by another is estimated at five years during which time there would be significant risk of dislocation, market volatility and loss of financial credibility.

By the 1960s Deutsch would describe the EC as a 'security community': an area in which people could form dependable expectations that change would only come about by peaceable means. This moral justification for European integration resembles the argument of the enlightenment philosopher Imanuel Kant, who believed that international society would civilise itself if only state power could be constrained for long enough – and in the right way – for a normative order to emerge between societies. It is interesting to arrive at a precise characterisation of how the EU has attempted such a strategy. Clearly the mere creation of trade interdependencies is not enough to constrain states to a consensual pattern of politics. Such economic contacts can be a source of friction rather than amity; and, as we are often reminded, intra-European trade at the moment of the outbreak of the First World War was at a highpoint (as a proportion of GNP) that would not be surpassed until the introduction of the EU's Single Market programme between 1986 and 1992 (Hirst and Thompson, 1996: 60).

The EU has attempted more radical change in the incentive structure of inter-state politics in at least four respects. First, the strategy has not just been to create a diffuse set of trading relationships but, as we have seen, to pinpoint key resources that would need to be mobilised in the event of conflict and place these beyond the unilateral control of individual governments. Second, even though the EU's Common Foreign and Security policy has often been modest, it has at least reduced the probability of member states engaging in uncoordinated alliance building with third countries. This is important because one way in which a group of states can fall out is where each feels compelled to underwrite the credibility of different sets of patron-client relations, as arguably happened when the Balkan crisis of 1914 turned into a general European conflict. Third, the absence of a strong European identity is besides the point; indeed, it could even be a regressive development in a Kantian strategy. Of far more importance is that various forms of national identity formation have been *de*-legitimised by European integration, conspicuously the holding of populations in continuous psychological readiness for conflict. As one military historian, has put it

> state power in the intensely competitive atmosphere of the late nineteenth century was military power, but military power involved the effective indoctrination of the entire population in a religion of nationalism; whatever the diverse and contested causes of war, it would, without all of this, have been far more difficult to mobilise European societies for conflict with one another.
>
> (Howard, 1983: 182)

Fourth, it is· vital to note that the restraining force of integration has worked through a mutually reinforcing combination of external and internal constraints on state power: in its dealings with its member states, and applicant states, the Union has privileged pluralist politics, democracy and the rule of law. The significance of this is that international contacts – such as trade – will only stabilise a regional order when those who benefit from them are able to form veto groups in each domestic political system; and this may, in turn, presuppose pluralist politics in which the rule of law is maintained by a complex order of checks and balances. This, interestingly enough, was precisely what Kant had in mind when he hoped that a family of *Rechtsstaaten* might one day live in 'universal peace' (Bull, 1977: 128).

This analysis yields some useful reflections on the general political legitimacy of supranational structures. We might, for example, regard these as justifiable where they are voluntary, rational and important to political equality. Not only have the member states voluntarily contracted to accept supranational constraints, this has often been seen as a rational act, for, paradoxically, these countries have found themselves in a position whereby they can only achieve the original goals and justifications of state power by placing certain limits on that power: they can only protect their populations (in a security order prone to 'prisoner's dilemma') by tying their own hands. What is more, the only alternative to collective self-limitation is that restrictions should be placed on particular member states, as was attempted with Germany in the interwar period. But such solutions may not command political legitimacy – the consent of the constrained – because they are regarded as discriminatory.

There are, however, two outstanding difficulties to the claim that the Union has been legitimated by delivery of security entitlements. Some argue that it is the disciplines of NATO and of an external hegemon – the US – that have kept European powers in order and that the Union itself would not have existed without this larger framework. Others suggest that the value of the Union's role may be time limited, or, put another way, the EU could find itself the victim of its own success. One interesting argument that developed during the Maastricht referendum in France was that European societies had evolved under the civilising umbrella of post-war institutions to a point of sophistication at which they would be ungovernable by any aggressor. Like the state in Marxist theory, the European Union had fulfilled its role in stabilising the security order and could now whither away, or turn to other tasks, such as the management of globalisation.

On other hand, the Union would appear if anything to be making tentative moves in the opposite direction, eroding the distinction, which we noted earlier, between a mere framework for the security of states and the direct provision of security itself. One view is that neither the Union nor its member states have full control over the definition of the EU's international roles, which are, to a degree, 'socially constructed' within the global arena. The Union may, for example, have reached a point in its political development at which it would be fatal to its credibility for it to allow an aggression against one of its member states. If this is so, it is already a security-provider to the extent that it offers an implicit security guarantee to its constituent countries (Hill, 1991: 292). The heavy criticism that the Union suffered during the Yugoslav crisis shows that there are some who would even extend this responsibility to neighbouring countries or to the European continent as a whole. A Union role might also be justified in terms of the inherently multilateral pattern of modern security provision and new forms of societal insecurity. On the first point, no European state has, arguably, had the capacity to function as an independent security provider since the 1940s. Defence planning has consistently had to assume partnerships in the event of conflict. Even where the Union does not recruit armies, it may be a crucial background factor in the brokering, and stabilisation, of security partnerships. This is precisely the argument that has been made for having a second pillar to the Union concerned with the *making* of a Common Foreign and Security Policy that may then be executed in other fora. On the second point, new patterns of insecurity often take the form of complex societal breakdowns – interactions between pathological communal conflicts, the delegitimation of power and economic dislocation – rather than states shifting armies across neatly defined political boundaries. Such breakdowns elsewhere in the world, have a potential to interact with new forms of internal insecurity facing EU countries, such as internationally organised crime, terrorism and immigration flows. Whereas the old style inter-state security threats of the cold war era were seen as justifying a simple multilateralism in which it was important that just one international organisation – NATO – should have undivided responsibility for security provision

(Kissinger, 1982), the new, more society-based, forms of insecurity are often thought to require 'multi-tasking', or access to several bodies, the Union included, each of which can enlarge the range of economic and diplomatic instruments available.

Economic and welfare rights delivery

The idea of economic *rights* is inherently problematic: it is hard for governments or other political processes to guarantee a set of economic or social outcomes; economic and social allocations tend to be the stuff of political competition in Western democracies, rather than the source of uncontested rights formation and fixed entitlements; and, of course, European countries run market econ-omies that are, to a certain extent, functionally dependent on economic *in*security and changeable rewards. Yet, of all the regions of the advanced industrial world, the societies that make up the EU have, arguably, seen the most ambitious accumulation of claims to deliver economic and welfare rights from within the political system; and, while there is much scope for disagreement on the exact definition of these entitlements, most would at least accept the negative conclusion that economic failure can be a powerful source of political *de*-legitimation.

It is unsurprising, therefore, that the fulfilment of economic and social needs has featured in previous justifications for power transfers to the European Union. The preamble to the Treaty of Rome has as one of its 'fundamental objectives . . . the constant improvement of the living and working conditions' of the 'peoples' of Europe (Treaty Establishing the European Community, 25 March, 1957). Subsequent documents have claimed that there is a distinctively European social model of entitlements that the Union exists, in part, to defend; for example, the Delors White Paper called for a radical overhaul of growth and employment policy on the grounds that this was needed to sustain embedded commitments to social cohesion and protection (Delors, 1994: II). While those Euro-sceptics who claim that the Union is an exclusively economic contract undoubtedly misrepresent the relationship, it is difficult to deny that membership has been sold on a heavily economic prospectus in several member countries. In the case of Britain, more speakers (both Labour and Conservative) in the House of Commons debates of July and October 1971 justified EC entry on the grounds that it would boost economic growth than for all other reasons put together (Lord, 1993: 102).

As with our discussion of security, one role for the EU in providing economic performance is the very general one of looking after systemic stability by heading off situations in which it may be individually rational for member states to do collectively irrational things (prisoners' dilemma). This may mean policing the trading system against competitive protection or devaluation, and the macro-economy against incompatible policy judgements. As Paul Hirst has remarked the idea of the ungoverned international economy has, historically, been something of a myth. The performance of the state, and the delivery of citizen expectations, has more often than not been dependent on transnational policy regimes: 'national policies have only been possible because of and within the constraints of an effective system of supranational economic governance' (Hirst, 1997: 413).

If this is so, and governments cannot avoid some kind of 'institution selection' in matters of transnational economic governance, the legitimacy of EU-based solutions will to a certain extent be a question of how they compare with alternatives. Apart from the option of non-governance (the inter-war period), the principal alternatives to Union responsibility would seem to be an external hegemon (US under Bretton Woods system, 1944–71); an internal hegemon (West Germany under the old ERM, 1979–93) or a global framework (G7). The latter may, however, be too diffuse, or it may presuppose some prior organisation of the world's economic regions with the implication that it is not really mutually exclusive with Union action. The case for a Union framework will, therefore, be two-fold: governance is better than non-governance; and shared management is fairer than an arrangement in which authorities from some states have far more influence over the regional economy than others. Interestingly the debate about Monetary Union has followed precisely these lines. The present initiative originates from the French and Italian Governments, who questioned the legitimacy of the existing economic order on the grounds that Union-wide policy was being made by a body – the Bundesbank – that was only empowered to consider the interests of one member society (Amato, 1988; Balladur, 1988).

Apart from providing a very general framework for stability, there are some who argue that the Union does not need to get involved in the direct delivery of economic and social entitlements;

and, indeed, that a demarcation of this kind might even be best for the legitimacy of both layers of political authority, national and European. To be precise, there are three arguments along these lines. Let us summarise each of them in turn before examining their validity:

I National policies represent non-generalisable social contracts

This argument might begin with the observation of several scholars that there are at least three different European models of capitalism and four kinds of welfare state. Amongst the different forms of welfare state, the original six members of the EU are said to follow a corporatist model in which social partners (employers and unions) play a considerable role in maintaining the system, and entitlements are designed to maintain the traditional family and acquired employment status of the individual; two of the three countries which joined in 1973 (UK and Ireland) are said to run a liberal model where entitlements are conceived as a minimum 'safety net'; the southern countries which joined in the 1980s (Spain, Portugal and Greece) run a somewhat patchy or *ad hoc* system which some regard as bordering on the clientelist; the Scandinavian countries, two of which joined in 1995, attempt a social democratic system designed to universalise the living standards and life chances of the middle class (De Jong, 1995; Esping-Andersen, 1990; Ferrera, 1996). Amongst models of capitalism, on the other hand, the main contrast is between the 'Anglo-Saxon' and 'Rhenish models' of finance capital: the latter presupposing far closer relationships between companies and providers of finance, and between governments, employers and unions in the management of the macro-economy (Rhodes, 1997: 171–9).

These differences create a fundamental problem for any attempt at direct delivery of economic and social entitlements through the EU: the very meaning of what constitutes good governing performance in socioeconomic rights delivery – and expectations of what it is appropriate for governments to do or not to do – will vary across the Union. On the one hand, this will make it difficult to agree 'one size fits all' policies at the Union level. On the other hand, any attempt to force national policies together may risk nationalistic counter-mobilisations, and break the rule that new political systems best establish their legitimacy by aligning their interests with pre-existing political elites (Sartori, 1988). Not the least reason for fearing this is that the welfare state has emerged as the main source of contact between nation states, their societies and citizenry, to the point, in some cases, of being a significant carrier of national identity and a principal *raison d'être* of national governance (Majone, 1993: 159). Common social and economic entitlements may also be unnecessary so long as variations in labour productivity continue to allow national governments to choose widely different levels of social welfare even in a frontier free market (Tsoukalis and Rhodes, 1997: 30). One view of the best strategy for the Union has, therefore, been expressed as follows: if market integration through the EU is used to provide an economic rescue of the nation state, but the Union otherwise keeps out of the direct provision of economic and social entitlements, the legitimacy of both Union and nation state is likely to increase (Milward, 1992); if, on the other hand, the EU involves itself in welfare provision both EU and nation state will move into a downward spiral of delegitimation, as the Union is seen to interfere with established patterns of entitlement, and it breaks a key link in the chain of loyalty between citizens and those national administrations upon which the Union itself depends for so many of its political resources.

2 The Union should confine itself to 'negative' integration

At the centre of this argument is a distinction between tearing down national restrictions to cross-border flows in Europe (negative integration) and the construction of common policy regimes at Union level (positive integration). It is sometimes suggested that the best way to establish the Union's legitimacy is to concentrate on the first and avoid the second. For, this, it is argued, avoids 'capabilities–expectations gaps' between ambitious economic responsibilities and the EU's narrow administrative resources; it prevents market structures and EU institutions developing in mutually pathological directions, as has arguably happened with the CAP; and, above all, it allows the outputs of the Union to be experienced as natural 'market forces', rather than the product of human agency in need of explicit legitimation. An interesting example of this point of view was provided by British counterproposals to the Delors Plan for Monetary Union. The UK Government argued that a Single Currency would command far more legitimacy if it evolved as a result of market choices between competing national currencies and/or a parallel European one; and less if it was imposed by EU institutions.

3 The Union should concentrate on making rules and avoid redistribution

This distinction is attributable to Majone's writings and is justified on the basis that the Union is not yet an integrated community with a shared sense of social responsibility (Majone in Richardson, 1996: 263). In the absence of the latter, redistribution between member societies may appear to be little better than theft. On the other hand, the Union may even be in a position to enjoy more legitimacy than the nation state in the making of certain rules that govern economic life. For, as we have seen, there are some rules that involve the adjudication of individual rights and which are, accordingly, best made or enforced by independent authorities (such as the Commission and the European Court of Justice), rather than elected majoritarian bodies (like member governments).

How valid are these arguments that the Union can – and ought – to abstain from the direct delivery of economic and social entitlements? We could begin by doubting whether they are sufficient to obscure all connection between Union power relations and individual life chances from public view, and then go on to observe that all of them involve questionable boundary relationships of one kind or another: between national and Union provision; between positive and negative integration; and between modes of economic governance. Doubts about the stability of any of these boundaries would subvert the argument that the Union can best ensure its legitimacy by confining itself to an arm's length role in economic and social rights delivery.

Far from negative integration disguising the role of power relations at the Union as 'natural' and apolitical market forces, it has, in the past, been an important moment when the Union has entered public consciousness. Not the least reason for this is that negative integration involves winners and losers, and transitional costs for both categories. It, therefore, requires explanation and purposeful organisation. A famous example was the impact of the Single Market on British politics. After years of attempting to insulate European Community membership from domestic politics, the Thatcher Government launched an intensive advertising campaign to persuade companies that Europe was now 'open for business'. This had the unintended consequence of transforming public awareness that the European Community was now a part of the governance structure of British society, important, on the admission of the Government itself, to continued economic well-being. As for the distinction between a Union based on rules, rather than redistributions, EU rules may even emerge as some of the most publicly visible steering mechanisms in domestic politics, as governments repeatedly appeal to them to bolster their own legitimacy and performance, or seek to internalise them to national administrative practice and private market behaviour. The classic example is the way in which they have used the criteria for entering a Monetary Union (maximum 3 per cent budget deficit and 60 per cent public debt) to provide domestic justification for restructuring public finances.

If, as this analysis suggests, publics become aware of the EU as much through negative as positive integration – or through rules as redistributions – two things may follow: first, publics, accustomed to mixed economies and, thus, to the idea that economic systems can be configured in many different ways, may begin to ask questions and require justifications as to what kind of economic and social justice EU is most likely to support; second, it may be hard for democratic governments to prevent publics from directing some of their own expectations of rights delivery towards the European arena. Thus Elizabeth Meehan shows how a series of measures that were originally intended as technical steps to remove market distortions – notably provisions on free movement of labour – have come to be refashioned in the public arena as 'rights' (Meehan, 1993). Sometimes, the two points may even come together; governments themselves need to take a lead in transferring social entitlements to the European level if they are to command sufficient consensus and citizen cooperation for various forms of market liberalisation. In other words, European frameworks often require the replication of social compromises that underpin domestic legitimation of economic governance. They cannot always be used to escape them, not least because European societies have evolved to a point of sophistication at which individual policy initiatives are easily exposed to cumulative delegitimation and under performance where they fail to achieve rapid and efficient compliance. For instance, the most recent IMF report notes that the cost of adjusting to the Maastricht criteria has been increased in several member states by a failure to convince publics that this was being done in a fair way (IMF report, September, 1997).

Nor is the distinction between negative and positive integration likely to be a stable one. Now there are many who argue that the reason for this is that the state becomes ineffective in a boundary less market with the result that the delivery of entitlements either has to be moved to the European level or abandoned altogether (Scharpf, 1997: 24). If true, this suggests a contradiction between the first and second of the foregoing arguments for keeping the Union out of the direct delivery of economic and social rights. For it may be impossible to use negative integration to rescue the nation state. Unless markets are complemented by an element of positive integration, a point will eventually be reached at which the welfare state will be unravelled by social dumping and the arbitrage of national systems of taxation and regulation.

However, we do not need to believe this story to arrive at the conclusion that negative integration would be unsustainable – or undesirable – without positive integration. The same conclusion could equally follow from the contrary assumption that states remain powerful actors in integrated markets. For, a combination of powerful states and a well integrated market is probably the worst possible outcome from the point of view of our earlier public choice analysis: such states would be very well placed to externalise harms to one another. Worse, patterns of victimisation would be unevenly distributed to the extent that European states, or social groups, differ in their capacity to convert market integration into a source of political power. Under such circumstances, negative integration may be seen as anything but a politically neutral force without need of legitimation. Take the relatively small example of the closure of a car factory at Vilvoorde in Belgium in spring 1997. Because Renault chose to shut this plant – although it was the most recently modernised – rather than one in France, many in Belgium suspected that there were some governments that the company needed to please more than others. The Union was widely criticised for creating a single market without matching institutions to protect citizens from unfair decisions. Support for integration in Belgium halved within a month.

A further difficulty is that a 'competitiveness state' (Cerny, 1997) – which survives negative integration by focusing its activities on the creation of competitive advantage – would be very different in its purpose and legitimacy to a welfare state. Under the latter, the public sphere is justified not just by its adaptiveness to market forces, but by its capacity to moderate them in the name of socially constructed notions of fairness. In addition to problems of social justice, patterns of risk in modern society may make it difficult to liberalise market relationships at European level without also constructing shared policy frameworks. Thus there is a case for moving banking supervision to the European level under a Monetary Union – and for harmonised regulation of pensions in integrated financial markets – because some risks are uninsurable, or the product of systemic collapse (contagious banking crises), or so devastating in their effects on individuals that compensation after the event is meaningless.

So, to summarise, we have suggested the following: that choices of economic system themselves require legitimation; that failure to provide this in terms of the justificatory principles of the societies concerned weakens the legitimacy of the political, as well as the economic, system; that the choices of economic system favoured by Union institutions are relatively easily discovered by the citizenry; and that complete abstention of the EU from any direct involvement in economic and social rights delivery would conflict with at least four sets of needs and values. First, with notions of *social justice*. Second, with the pattern of *risk* in the economic and social systems concerned. Third, with the *embeddedness* of entitlements – the way in which they have been factored into individual life plans beyond easy adjustment. And fourth, the role of such entitlements in underpinning *consensus* in systems that depend upon sophisticated forms of citizen collaboration.

But this only suggests that the Union cannot legitimate itself by concentrating on negative integration alone. Positive integration could still create legitimation problems of a different kind. Writing in the 1970s, Jürgen Habermas argued that the tendency for liberal democratic political systems to assume responsibility for market failures was a recurrent source of crisis tendencies; the state was turned into a dumping ground for problems that it could only meet by drawing on deep reserves of political legitimacy, not least because the correction of market failures would often bring it into conflict with the organising principles of capitalist reproduction (Habermas, 1976). Now this underestimates the capacity of the state to play down, rather than meet, economic expectations (Beetham, 1991). But, that said, any growth in EU responsibility for the correction of market failures would involve a kind of double displacement of problems; from market to state and from state to the European Union. The difficulty here is that the EU has very different reserves of legitimacy to any found at national level. On the one hand, its performance might be superior to the extent that it is able to deal with transnational – or more systemic – forms of market failure; on the other, it has little direct democratic authority. Although, it can, of course, draw on the legitimacy of its member states, this is differentially established in matters of economic governance. Moreover, as we have repeatedly seen, governments may be more interested in off loading difficulties and shifting blame than in supporting the Union in its problem-solving capacity.

Civic/legal rights delivery

Entitlements that typically fall into this category include equality before the law and rights that guarantee the meaningful participation of the citizen in civil society and in the democratic process. Now, it might be thought that European integration has little to offer here; that the entitlements in question were well established within the domestic arena before the EU came along; that unlike the two categories we have just reviewed, they do not depend upon any kind of international systemic stability; and that they can never be satisfactorily delivered through a non-state political system because they depend on a monopoly of violence. On the other hand, the EU clearly has developed a role in this area. The early rulings of the ECJ in the 1960s established that the obligations of membership had direct effect on individuals and that no political system could rightfully impose duties without also conferring rights (Meehan, 1993). During the 1990s, the notion of Union citizenship has become an important part of the Union's pitch for legitimation. In the preamble to the Treaty of European Union the signatories resolve 'to establish a citizenship common to nationals of all countries' (European Communities, 1992), and the Amsterdam Treaty claims that the 'Union is founded on the principle of liberty, democracy, respect for human rights and fundamental freedoms'. It then goes on to formalise the competence of the European Court of Justice in questions of fundamental rights, giving it the right to proceed against Union institutions in this regard, and even to take sanctions against the member states themselves. By a majority vote, the Council will be able suspend the membership rights of a recalcitrant state, including its voting rights. As the likely benchmark in all of this will be the various human rights charters of the Council of Europe, the new Union Treaty may represent the effective convergence of the two streams of supranational civil rights delivery in postwar Europe. In the public mind, however, the two may long have been linked in a single expectation that it is possible for the individual to 'go to Europe' to enforce certain rights against the state.

How do we explain and justify these developments? It is by no means self-evident that a European framework should produce better delivery of civic–legal rights than relying on the nation state alone. The rise of pluralism and liberal constitutionalism has, after all, been attributed to the 'avoidance of Empire': to the existence of a multiple state system in which the oppressive have failed to nurture or retain talent with the result that they have, in the long run, lost out in the process of competition between political systems (Gellner, 1994; Hall, 1985). We have already stumbled across part of the answer for why a competitive states system may be inadequate; the way in which international breakdowns can spill over to affect various forms of internal rights. Take, for example, Eric Hobsbawm's description of the inter-war period:

> In 1918–20 legislative assemblies were dissolved or became ineffective in two European states, in the 1920s in six, the 1930s nine, while German occupation destroyed constitutional power in another five during the Second World War. In short, the only countries with adequately democratic institutions that functioned without a break during the entire inter-war period were Britain, Finland (only just), the Irish free state, Sweden and Switzerland. The region experienced an accelerating, increasingly catastrophic collapse of democratic institutions. (Hobsbawm, 1994: 111)

In these circumstances, it has been useful for the Union to offer a kind of double guarantee against abuse of rights, though, of course, that very notion implies that it should not itself aspire to a monopoly of rights provision. Some view the Union as reinforcing civic entitlements by making the national arena more transparent to critical comparisons with the result that each government comes under pressure to justify the denial of rights that exist elsewhere in the Union. However, there are at least two other factors at work. One is that the Union may be a peculiarly suitable institution for the nesting of a double guarantee of certain civic rights. On the one hand, rulings of the ECJ benefit from the fact that governments have invested too heavily in a viable Union to depart too far or too often from a pattern of self-enforcement of the rules. On the other hand, the Union is too dependent on cooperation of member states for it to become monopolistic itself in the definition of civic rights. A second factor is a kind of normative spill-over. It is simply very hard for the Union to concern itself with major areas of public policy – not to mention such matters as justice and home affairs – without it reaching an agreed view on appropriate relationships between the individual and public authority.

Interactions with the national dimension

Throughout this chapter we have argued that there has been an intimate interdependence in the performance of the Union and its member states to the point at which they are in the 'same boat' when it comes to that dimension of legitimation. However, the character of this mutual dependence varies across states.

National dependence on the EU for effective governing performance

In this section we identify three clusters of reasons why the performance of member states depends on the European framework to different degrees: the first concerns size, resources and the character of boundary erosions; the second, differences in political sensitivity and vulnerability; and the third, differences in belief about legitimacy itself.

There are good reasons why smaller states may have special need for an effective Union. With large export and import dependencies and narrow home markets, these countries would lose most from an erosion of the European trading system and from loss of politically guaranteed access to larger economies. In the past, they have also been victims of breakdowns in the European security order, not least because a structure of small states sandwiched between large ones is amongst the most unstable in any balance of power system. Belgium illustrates both points perfectly. On the economic side, it trades more with other countries than itself; and, on the security side, it has, historically, often been turned into the battlefield of Europe.

Even where small states do not want to join supranational structures, they may find that their performance is seriously undermined by decisions of large states to do so. Amongst the original six, The Netherlands was something of a reluctant participant in the Schuman Plan of 1950, anxious about the new supranational institutions, but unable to risk its entrepot trade to other European markets. In 1973, Denmark and Ireland were dragged into the European Community in the wake of British accession. And the Single Market programme of 1986–92 made it very difficult for the remaining small states of West Europe to remain aloof from the Union (Wallace and Wessels, 1991: 269–70). The down side of this, however, is that the relationship of some small states with the EU may be seen as something of a shot-gun marriage; and the loss of an intimate political arena always has to be set against new advantages of scale. A further problem is the ambiguity with which the EU distributes power between large and small states; while it over-represents the smaller states in its formal decision-making structures, there is always a suspicion that the larger members dominate informal bargaining relationships.

Turning to differences of wealth and development, poorer states may find that citizen expectations of good governing performance are conditioned by comparisons with some 'European average' that they have no hope of resourcing internally. If autarky is to be excluded, such countries often need the help of European frameworks to advance their development. For example, the Single Market programme is thought to facilitate capital imports – needed to break out of the constraints of limited domestic surplus – by offering politically credible guarantees that investments will be returned at a later date; and the EU's structural funds have been used to make investments in infrastructure and human resources. For some countries, notably the new Mediterranean democracies, aspects of state formation itself have followed from Union membership, rather than been anterior to it. Some policies, institutions and laws have been adopted wholesale from the EU or other member countries.

No member state – even the largest – can be characterised as even approximating to a closed economy or society. However, there are clear variations in the extent and character of boundary erosions, and the manner in which these interact with accumulated political commitments. An interesting example is provided by cooperation on questions of justice and home affairs. Take the narcotics trade, which presents much the same problem to all member states; it is organised in international networks, it supports other forms of criminality and it filters into the legitimate economy through activities like money laundering. Yet, in spite of this, the Schengen agreement has produced what is at first sight a rather peculiar membership. Although it does not include two member states – Britain and Ireland – it does now embrace two non-members, Norway and Iceland. On closer inspection, however, this can be explained by differences in the character of boundary erosions. Without land frontiers, mainland Britain still has some chance of effectively policing its external frontier. Irish Governments may feel more sympathetic to Schengen but could only subscribe to it by breaking their free travel area with the UK, which is very important given the demographic flows of its citizenry. Conversely, Norway and Iceland have had to be included (even though the latter would seem to be even better placed than the UK to defend its external frontier) because they are already signed up to free movement agreements with two EU states – Denmark and Sweden – that have felt too exposed to the drug trade to do without the help of Schengen (Cullen, 1995: 65–91).

Even where a country is substantially penetrated from outside, it may, however, feel little need for European policy frameworks. To use Robert Keohane and Joseph Nye's distinction, they may be either insensitive or invulnerable or both: the first is where cross-border flows do not matter enough to become politically salient; the second is where a state can avoid a collaborative response because it has every prospect of doing rather well out of a 'non-cooperation game' (Keohane and Nye, 1977). A classic example of the latter is provided by the old Exchange Rate Mechanism of the European Monetary System. Even France and Italy – respectively the fourth and sixth largest western economies and both members of the G7 – could not make this relationship 'symmetrical' between themselves and Germany. Because Germany always enjoyed greater policy credibility it was comparatively 'invulnerable' and often well placed to compel the other two to bear a disproportionate share of policy adjustments. The result was that it was unclear what interest Germany could possibly have in the further intensification of collaboration to the point of full Monetary Union, apart, of course, from broader commitment to integration and geopolitical adjustment to a new Europe.

But even this does not get to the heart of the matter. What often makes the key difference in how the EU interacts with domestic governing performance is the nature of belief in legitimacy itself; things are a good deal easier in those countries where European integration reinforces justificatory principles for the exercise of political power in the domestic arena. In the case of Germany, for example, constraint on political power is an important component of its legitimacy; the supranational constraints that the Union places on the German state may even make it more legitimate in much the same way as the federal structure, *Rechtsstaat* and consensus party system are regarded as doing so. An adage that is often employed in German politics is that Germany brought ruin on itself when it attempted to develop its international power unilaterally; in contrast, it has prospered by accepting the disciplines of multilateral frameworks such as the EU. In Britain, on the other hand, majority control of the absolute and inalienable sovereignty of the Westminster Parliament is seen as legitimating government. This causes immense problems for Britain in the EU and may well, indirectly, restrict the contributions that integration can make to effective governing performance in the UK. For, with the exception of the Single Market initiative of 1985, British Governments have often been too absorbed in the management of domestic opposition to set the Union agenda to their own advantage. The result has been to confirm the ascendancy of the Franco-German *force motrice*, even though President Pompidou purposefully brought Britain in to the Community to create a more balanced triangular relationship (Lord, 1993).

Dependence of EU on national systems

If there are deep reasons of political legitimation why the executive structures of national and Union governance need to be fused, then the performance of the Union will clearly be affected by differences in the politics of its member states. Given that it has not yet taken deep roots in public sentiment, the Union probably comes closer than most institutions to Weber's belief that legitimacy is primarily a question of the loyalty and commitment of elites, though with the curious proviso that the elites in question are those of another set of political systems. National administrative machines service the Presidency of the Council of Ministers and participate in the empire of *ad hoc* committees through which so much Union policy is made. They are also responsible for enforcing Union law and, where implementation gaps arise, it is often because domestic elites question the legitimacy of a particular Union measure to the point of believing that they are entitled to continue their opposition by the alternative means of prevarication (Richardson, 1996). Now, at first sight, it would seem that the commitment of elites to the effective working of the Union is very high and that this is true across all member states and types of elite (political, administrative, business and media). However, as Table 2.2 shows, this disguises familiar differences in what national elites consider to be legitimate methods of integration.

In any case, we have consistently argued that the commitment of elites can never be enough to legitimate a political system. One reason for this is that a national elite can be committed but incapable or dishonest to the point at which it discredits the Union and complicates its performance (Peterson, 1997). Another is that commitment may only reflect deeper characteristics of domestic political systems. In a world in which elites adjust to the requirements of successful competition for political power, it is a fair surmise that the identity of the median voter or of the marginal party to any act of coalition formation will colour overall approaches to European integration. This may be true even where European issues are not salient. For they may be indirectly important to the delivery of those things that do matter to swing voters and parties. Now the identity of median voters or marginal party actors is conditioned by the rules of the political system. We have, for instance, already seen how adversarial one-party government made it far more difficult for a dominant pro-European coalition to emerge amongst Britain's ruling elite than was the case in other member states between 1973 and 1997. Nonetheless, it is not entirely clear whether this has adversely affected the performance of the Union. British Governments have been fairly thorough implementors of Union law and have not succeeded in blocking a considerable expansion in both the competence and supranational powers of the Union. Some even argue that British hostility has been a catalyst to integration, cementing alliances that would not otherwise hold (Camps, 1964; Lawson, 1992). A more measured analysis is that the hostility of one member state cannot compromise the performance of the Union where the others are able to threaten 'alternative coalitions': where they are able to convince the laggard that they are able to move ahead alone and then impose certain externalities on the outsider or force it into the initiative on worse terms than would have secured by collaborating in consensus formation in the first place (Moravcsik, 1993).

Implications for the shape of the EU's political system

What implications do considerations of EU performance have for the shape of its institutions? Once again, we could usefully take public choice theory as our starting point, before going on to acknowledge some of its limitations. Just as public choice theory has been used to justify patterns of policy assignment to the Union on grounds of governing performance, it has also been employed to reach conclusions as to how power, once transferred to the EU, should be most legitimately distributed across its institutions. A typical starting point is with the observation that some public goods can be provided by informal clubs and with a minimum of institutional commitment. Where this is the case, it may be sufficient for member states to coordinate their activities in the Council of Ministers, without ceding extensive powers to centralised and supranational structures. However, independent institutions will be needed where there are high transaction costs in reaching agreement or information is imperfect (Coase, 1960; Majone in Richardson, 1996: 69; Inman and Rubinfeld, 1997: 76). From this apparently anodyne observation a whole stream of justifications for the political powers of the Commission and European Court of Justice might follow: the need for an impartial agenda-setter where there is a risk of member states spending so much time arguing about the 'distribution of value' that they fail to create it (Sebenius, 1992; Pollack, 1997): the value of employing specialist supranational agencies to fill in subsequent details of agreements that are, of their very nature, likely to be 'incomplete contracts', vague at the moment they are negotiated between states (Williamson, 1985; Majone in Richardson, 1996: 43–4); the need for independent enforcers if states are to solve 'time inconsistency problems' and commit themselves credibly to carrying out agreements that may be to the temporary inconvenience of particular governments (Kydland and Prescott, 1977; Majone in Richardson, 1996: 41–2).

Public choice perspectives might also justify a further peculiarity of the EU's political system: the practice of flexible integration. In spite of the *acquis communautaire* doctrine that all commitments should apply equally across the Union, the EU has often been at its most innovative in finding ways to apply its policies differentially; derogations, opt-outs, transition periods and constructive abstention are but a few of the best known devices (Wallace and Ridley, 1985). Even flexible integration itself has been flexibly conceptualised in three different modes (Stubb, 1996); complete freedom to dip in and out of policies (*à la carte*); proceeding at different speeds to the same objective (multi-speed), and durable differences in the membership of policy regimes (variable geometry). Now, the problem with this is that uniformity of rights and obligations may be important to the legitimacy of a political system: first, because it is related to fairness; and, second, because a system that is shot through with exceptions may not command authority or even autonomy.

Yet, some might continue to argue that uniformity of rights and obligations can be a necessary condition for legitimacy at the national level without this being true at the European. First the EU is in the peculiar position that its membership is a mixture of states and individuals, and we may find it easier to accept that states should have different rights and obligations than that individuals should do so, especially if such differences have been voluntarily contracted. Second, states may differ so widely in their need and preference for European integration that flexible approaches are 'utility maximising': the benefits of insisting on uniform application would, according to this point of view, be greatly outweighed by the costs of holding some countries back and forcing others forward.

However, there are a couple of problems with all this. First, it may be very difficult to strike flexible bargains between states without creating discriminatory patterns of entitlement between individuals. Thus Britain's opt-out from the social chapter amounted to saying that British employees were signed up to a political system that was prepared to deliver rights to others but not to them. Second, if we really were to believe that transnational institutions should be flexibly developed, in order to maximise utility, we might not expect a European Union to emerge at all. The original functional theories of international integration thus anticipated a whole series of international authorities, as each issue would generate a geographically different 'optimal policy-making area' (Mitrany, 1943). More contemporary public choice perspectives might get round this problem by stressing the advantages of 'nesting' flexible integration in the general normative order of the EU (Tsebelis, 1990). But that is halfway to conceding that institutions create their own legitimation and that 'form' does not, therefore, ineluctably follow function.

Indeed, let us return to our own preferred position that legitimation by performance is not just about efficiency solutions. To recapitulate from the introductory section, it is also about history and perception; it can never be fully detached from our other two criteria for legitimation, democracy and identity; and above all it can be partially created, or lost, within the very institutional relationships it is supposed to legitimate. Now, we believe, all of this can be used to yield a far more convincing account of why the relationship between legitimacy and performance is likely to be unique in the case of the EU. It is, as we have repeatedly seen, because the EU has had to begin by piggy-backing on the democratic legitimacy and established political identities of member states that it has had to develop through political and administrative fusion with its member states. But this has, in turn, imposed its own 'path-dependence' on the legitimation of the Union. It has, on the one hand, left it with far less power than other political systems to develop its own self-fulfilling criteria for performance and legitimation; on the other, it is more exposed to blame shifting and unreasonable problem displacement from 'lower' levels of government.

Fusion has also endowed the Union with a unique set of institutional qualities and pathologies. The extreme consensus democracy to which it gives rise may aid performance where there is much to be gained from policy learning and there is plenty of time to make decisions. It can also be effective where there is a great deal of scope to make decisions that leave everyone better off (positive-sum games), or failing that, where package deals can be coherently constructed and democratically defended. But it works badly where these conditions do not apply. One interesting implication of all this is that the Union often works well where public choice perspectives would predict that it would perform badly, and vice versa. To return to our example of fishing, we saw earlier that it offers a classic example of how market failure justifies the need for a public policy regime. Yet, all public bodies, the Union included, have had remarkable difficulty establishing the legitimacy of their interventions, probably because fishing is conducted by small, relatively closed, communities where passions run high and sacrifices involve entire loss of livelihood. In other words, it is just one of those zero-sum games that you would not expect the Union to be able to handle in its consensus based institutions. On the other hand, the Union has had conspicuous successes in dealing with urban water pollution. This has nothing to do with cross border problems: there is no transnational externality involved. But Environment Departments have often worked through the Union – even where it is not strictly necessary for them to do so – because it allows them to learn from each other and escape the constraints of domestic governments where they are usually over-ruled by Trade and Industry Departments (Sbragia, 1996).

Conclusion

Legitimacy through performance is a combination of two distinct elements: some measure of public agreement on the criteria to be attained; and the evident institutional capacity to attain them. As to the first, we have seen how attempts have been made to justify a Union-level framework with reference to three kinds of rights delivery; rights to physical security, economic and social welfare and to certain civic liberties. More minimalist definitions of EU functions have been shown to be unsustainable. As to the second, we have argued that the Union will not be able to achieve better results than the nation state merely because it is better adapted to the 'problem structure', whether by virtue of scale or cross-border effects. Better performance will also be a question of institutions and their capacity, and the difficulty here is that the EU's political system is constrained by our other two dimensions of legitimation. Problems with identity formation and democratisation at the Union require idiosyncratic approaches to decision making that have powerful knock-on effects to the overall performance of the Union. This brings us back to the interaction between different dimensions of legitimacy, which we will now develop further in our concluding chapter.

CHAPTER FIVE

Legitimacy in the EU – problems and prospects

In this volume we have been exploring some of the central debates and issues about the EU through the conceptual lens of 'political legitimacy'. How useful is this concept, and what can it offer that other conceptual approaches cannot, or not so well? The starting point of any discussion of legitimacy is the simple observation that all government is involved in producing binding rules and regulations for those under its authority, and in distributing burdens and benefits between them; and that, since these activities involve coercion, restrictions on liberty and the imposition of material costs on people, they require substantial justification, both in terms of by what and whose authority government so acts, and what broader purposes and values are served by its doing so. Whether we call such justifications moral, prescriptive, normative, or whatever, is a matter of terminological preference. What makes them important is that they engage us both as individuals with our own interests and purposes to pursue, and also as moral agents who expect our social and political arrangements to conform to some standard of the right and the good, however imperfectly they may do so in practice.

Usually we may not bother our heads with such questions, but take them for granted and go about our daily business regardless. Yet once these justifications for political authority become seriously challenged within a society, or its institutions of government manifestly fail to meet the justificatory criteria expected of them, then we are forced to reflect about these questions. And then we discover something else: that what political authority is capable of achieving, and even its capacity to function at all, or to do so without substantial change, is dependent on its moral standing among those whose support or cooperation is needed for it to achieve its purposes, whether these be key elites or the public at large. Something of this kind became evident in the UK in September 1997, when the moral standing of the monarchy, already in decline, was crucially undermined by its reaction to the death of Princess Diana, and a gulf became evident between the Queen and the people, on whose support her authority was now seen to depend. In this case the questioning of political legitimacy heralded the end, not so much of the monarchy itself, as of a particular kind of monarchy.

Such a condition of 'forced reflection' about the justification for political authority could be said to be a chronic one for the European Union; the question of its legitimacy is continuously present. This is so for a number of reasons, which we have explored in this volume. First and most obvious is that the EU, in its exercise of direct legislative and regulatory authority, and in its redistribution of burdens and benefits between groups of citizens as well as countries, challenges our received assumption that the rightful source of such authority lies with the people constituted as a nation, rather than cross-nationally; and that the rightful locus for these authoritative rules and allocations should be the familiar institutions of the nation state. To be sure, the nation state in Europe has been partially delegitimised through the course of the twentieth century: two intra-European wars have demonstrated that a system of sovereign nation states, each pursuing their interests independently, is incapable of guaranteeing the physical security of their respective citizens; while developments in the global economy have put many of the determinants of people's economic welfare beyond the reach or decisional capacity of domestic governments. Such deficiencies in the ability of the nation state to meet the very basic purposes of government – security and welfare – lie at the heart of any justification for European institutions.

Yet for all these limitations the nation state retains a decisive pull on the loyalty of its citizens, and a formative influence on their political identities, through the organisation of linguistic, cultural and educational life at the national level. In contrast the idea of Europe, and of a common identity shared by peoples of such different traditions and historical experiences, seems remarkably tenuous by comparison, especially when membership of this entity is continually changing. Here lies a major gap: between the political requirement for a governmental authority beyond the nation state, and the popular loyalty needed to support that authority. This gap could be seen as one of the respective speeds of different social processes – institutional construction on the one hand, and cultural change on the other. In comparison with the former, the latter is relatively slow, sometimes generational, and cannot be subject to simple control or manipulation. It is as if the nation state is over-supplied with loyalty and the EU undersupplied, and some rebalancing is needed. Yet this above all requires time, and in the meantime the imbalance provides the locus for recurrent doubt and questioning.

A second reason why the issue of the EU's legitimacy is continu-ously in play is that the scope of its authority is subject to repeated change, as it takes on ever new tasks which were previously the monopoly of member states. Whether this extension of scope should be attributed to the push of committed 'Europhiles', the pull of a functionalist logic of 'spillover' from existing tasks, or the inherent dynamic of a system which, like the cyclist, has to keep moving forward to stay upright, need not detain us here; at all events it is a process which encourages continual questioning. What should governments be doing, individually and collectively? At what level, and through what arrangements, can they do so most effectively? The development of the EU makes these questions matters of ongoing debate and often open contestation. Political disagreements – between Left and Right, modernisers and tradition-alists, etc. – which are the ordinary stuff of politics at the level of the nation state, become transposed at the European level into support or opposition to EU institutions themselves: a matter of the legitimacy of their authority as such, not merely of normal political debate within it.

At the same time there is recurrent questioning about the effec-tiveness of EU institutions in achieving the purposes assigned to them, at the level of both decision making and enforcement. At the level of decision making, there is a constant tension between the need for rules and policies that are uniform, coherent and practicable, and the need to be sensitive to national differences and particularities; a tension that is reflected in the enormous complexity of the decision-making process itself. At the level of enforcement, the necessity of leaving this key function to the enforcement agencies of member states renders the EU vulnerable to potentially wide variations in competence and determination between the respective agencies, and to loss of credibility in regu-lative authority as a consequence. So in the attainment of its distinctive purposes, which is the prime justification for the EU, its performance remains open to question.

A third reason why the legitimacy of the EU is subject to questioning, as we have shown, lies in the widespread perception of a deficiency in its democratic credentials: by whom its decision makers are authorised, to whom they are accountable and in what sense they are representative. The common characterisation of the EU as 'bureaucratic' – secretive, unaccountable and beyond popular reach – is expressive of this disquiet. On the one hand, EU decision making has evolved beyond the point where it can be effectively rendered accountable at the national level, to national parliaments and publics; while the institutional arrangements for ensuring authorisation and accountability at the European level are still underdeveloped, on the other. Even were they more developed, there would remain the question of whether there yet exists an 'attentive public', apart from particular interest groups, to provide the necessary impetus for accountability and representation, and which would be needed to make democratic institutions work in practice. Democracy after all is not only a matter of arrangements, but of effective popular agency.

These recurrent questions about the rightfulness of the EU's authority – its source, extent and mode of institutionalisation – can be thematised analytically through the concept of legitimacy 'deficit' or 'deficits': the idea of a gap between the moral authority or normative standing *required* by a public authority engaged in the production of binding rules and allocations, and that which it is *actually able* to command. In analysing this gap or deficit, we have found it necessary to take into account a number of different dimensions of complexity. Three of these dimensions can be distinguished for purposes of review.

The first dimension of complexity involves the distinction between an indirect and a direct mode of legitimation; between a legitimacy that derives from member states and has their own politico-economic elites as addressees or 'audience', and a legitimacy that derives from their citizens and engages them directly. We have argued that the indirect mode, typical of international or intergovernmental organisations, is inadequate for the kind of governmental functions exercised by the EU, which affect the lives of citizens directly. Yet the indirect mode cannot simply be abandoned while nations and their political institutions retain such a strong focus of loyalty, and the constitution of a European public is still only embryonic.

At first sight it would appear as if here lies one obvious solution to any legitimacy deficit: the direct and indirect modes might be complementary and mutually reinforcing, reflecting a balance between the supranational and intergovernmental elements in the EU's institutional arrangements. Might not, say, the deficiency in accountability of EU decision making to national parliaments be remedied by accountability to the European Parliament and the weakness of a European identity be remedied by strong national support for EU institutions and identifiable national representation on them? The problem, however, is whether this complexity is not as much a source of incoherence as of mutual reinforcement. To take the example of accountability, it is doubtful whether two forms of accountability coexisting, the direct and indirect, each of which on its own is inadequate, add up to an adequate one, and one which is not confusing to the relevant publics. In the case of loyalty and identity, these may be conflictual as well as complementary, as national identities are emphasised at the expense of European; or the logic of direct popular authorisation of key EU officials, which is subject to the criteria of personality and programme, runs counter to the logic of indirect authorisation, in which considerations of national identity and interest are supreme. What at first sight looks like a compatibility or mutual reinforcement between two modes of legitimacy, the direct and indirect, can thus simply result in incoherence.

A second dimension of complexity, and one that has been central to the organisation of this book, involves the three normative criteria of legitimacy – identity, democracy and performance, respectively – and the interaction between them. We have seen that two different accounts of this interaction are possible. One is the idea of *compensation*: a deficiency in one of the criteria can be compensated for by another. Thus a deficiency in democracy can be compensated for by performance, and vice versa. In the case of the EU, performance has always been the lead element in its legitimation: the justification both for its existence and for its decisional scope lies in the inadequacies in what the nation state can achieve on its own. And, as we have seen, this emphasis on performance translates readily into a technocratic account of the EU's legitimacy. Yet there are also clear limits to the compensatory capacity, if it may be so called, of the performance criterion of legitimacy. Where it is the only normative basis for political authority, the latter becomes exceedingly vulnerable to performance failure. Moreover, as we have seen, decisions over conflicting values, and the priority between them, can only be resolved by appeal to an ultimate source of authority, which in European societies can now only be to the people. It is precisely these limits to performance as legitimator that has provided one of the main imperatives to democratisation of the EU, and to encouraging a more European focus for political identity.

At this point a rather different account of the interaction between our three criteria becomes appropriate. This involves the idea of *displacement*: resolving a deficit in one area displaces the problem onto another. So resolving a performance problem by extending the EU's scope into functionally adjacent areas, or by the increased use of majority voting in the Council of Ministers, exacerbates the democratic deficit by further weakening account- ability to national parliaments. And reducing this democratic deficit by strengthening direct authorisation and accountability within EU institutions exposes in turn the very limited development of a public arena, or a popular identity and loyalty at the European level. Analysis of the legitimacy deficit is thus not just a question of identifying the problems in the three different areas, in our three normative criteria, but of understanding the process of inter- action between them.

A further dimension of complexity that we have identified in our analysis of legitimacy involves the impact of EU institutions on the political legitimacy of member states, and vice versa. Once again, two different versions of this interaction can be given, one optimistic, the other less so. The optimistic version sees the develop- ment of the EU as strengthening the legitimacy of member states, by narrowing their performance scope to functions that are within their competence, and strengthening the policy environment in those areas that are now beyond them. Not surprisingly, the optimistic version concentrates on the performance criterion. Even here, however, it overlooks the negative impact on the EU of being identified as the source of blame for failures of policy at the national level, or simply for unpopular decisions which have to be made at some level or other. And no account is taken of the effect of EU institutions in intensifying the deficit of democratic account- ability at the national level, or in the explicit erosion of national sovereignties, both of which in turn affect public perceptions of political legitimacy at the European level. So there are potentially vicious as well as virtuous circles at work between the two levels, though, as we have also shown, these also vary between different member states and different constituencies within them. It is precisely to address such variation that proposals for a 'multi-speed' Europe, 'variable geometry' and national opt-outs have been seriously entertained.

In conclusion, then, the argument of the book is that the issue of legitimacy and the EU is a complex one, but it is not a complexity that defies analysis. The key to its analysis lies in an understanding of the different dimensions in which legitimacy is constructed and reproduced, and of the interactions within them: between a direct and an indirect mode of legitimation; between our three normative criteria (performance, identity, democracy); and between political authority at the national and European levels respectively. As we have also argued, there are good reasons for concluding that a merely optimistic account of these different dimensions is misconceived: that the direct and indirect modes are mutually conflictual as much as complementary; that there is displacement at work as well as compensation between our three criteria; that the two levels of public authority in the European political space may be undermining of each other's legitimacy as well as mutually reinforcing of it.

It is because an optimistic reading of these different dimensions is inadequate that the legitimacy of EU institutions is continuously open to question, and that we are justified in talking of a legitimacy deficit or deficits at the European level. Yet these are not something merely *given* in the order of things, like an event of nature, in the face of which collective action is powerless. In this sense we have also talked of them as dilemmas, which can be more or less successfully managed by public policy. And managing them itself contributes to the process of political change. If we consider the dimensions outlined above, then a process of change in the EU can be charted from the indirect towards the more direct mode of legitimation; from performance as the sole justificatory criterion towards issues of democracy and identity; from inter-European elites to national populations as the addressees of legitimacy claims. Such change marks a shift, not only in the locus of legitimacy deficits, but in the agenda of problems for future negotiation and resolution also.

References

Abelès, M. (1992). *La Vie Quotidienne au Parlement Européen*, Paris: Hachette.

Amato, G. (1988). *Un motore per lo SME*, 25 February, 1998, Rome: *Il Sole 24 Ore*.

Anderson, B. (1991). *Imagined Communities: Reflections on the Origin and Spread of Nationalism*, London: Verso.

Andeweg, R. (1995). The reshaping of national party systems, *West European Politics*, **18**, 3, 58–78.

Andolfanto, D. (1994). Les Euro-Députés en question, *Revue Politique el Parlementaire*, Mars–Avril, No. 970.

Arrow, K. (1963). *Social Choice and Individual Values*, New York: Wiley.

Attinà, F. (1990). The voting behaviour of European Parliament members and the problem of the Europarties, *European Journal of Political Research*, **17**, 557–79.

Attina, F. (forthcoming) Party fragmentation and discontinuity in the European Union, in D. Bell and C. Lord (eds) *Transnational Parties in the European Union*, Aldershot: Ashgate.

Baier, A. (1995). *Moral Prejudices: Essays on Ethics*, Cambridge, MA: Harvard University Press.

Balladur, E. (1988). *La Construction Monétaire Européenne*, Paris: Ministère des Finances et de l'Économie.

Bardi, L. (1994). Transnational party federations, European parliamentary party groups and the Building of Europarties, in R. Katz and P. Mair (eds) *How Parties Organise: Adaptation and Change in Party Organisations and Western Democracies*, 1960–90, London: Macmillan.

Barker, R. (1990). *Political Legitimacy and the State*, Oxford: Clarendon Press.

Bauman, Z. (1997). *Postmodernity and its Discontents*, Cambridge: Polity.

Begg, I and Grimwade, N. (1997). Economic and budgetary challenges, in G. Edwards, and A. Pijpers (eds), *The 1996 Intergovernmental Conference and Beyond,* London: Pinter.

Beetham, D. (1991). *The Legitimation of Power*, Basingstoke: Macmillan.

Beetham, D. (1996). *Bureaucracy*, 2nd edn, Buckingham: Open University Press.

Bieber, R. and Monar, J. (1996). *Justice and Home Affairs in the European Union: The Development of the Third Pillar*, Bruxelles: European Interuniversity.

Bogdanor, V. (1986). The future of the EC: two models of democracy, *Government and Opposition*, 21, 2, 161–76.

Bogdanor, V. (1996). The European Union, the political class and the people, in J. Hayward (1996) *Elitism, Populism and European Politics*, Oxford: Clarendon Press.

Bogdanor, V. (1998). *Financial Times*, 5 January, 1998.

Bull, H. (1977). *The Anarchical Society: A Study of Order in World Politics*, Basingstoke: Macmillan.

Bullen, R. and Pelly, M. (1986). The Schuman Plan, The Council of Europe and Western European Integration, Documents on British Policy Overseas, II, 1.

Buzan, B. (1991). *People, States and Fear: An Agenda for International Security Studies in the Post Cold War Era*, Hemel Hempstead: Harvester Wheatsheaf.

Caporaso, J.A. (1996). The European Union and forms of state: Westphalian, regulatory or post-modern?, *Journal of Common Market Studies*, 34, 1, 29–52.

Calvoceressi, C. and Wint, G. (1972). *Total War: Causes and Courses of the Second World War*, Harmondsworth: Penguin.

Camps, M. (1964). *Britain and the European Community, 1955–1963*, Princeton: Princeton University Press.

Carr, E. (1964). *The Twenty Year Crisis*, New York: Harper Row.

Cederman, L-E. (1996). Nationalism and integration: Merging two literatures in one framework, Oslo: European Consortium for Political Research.

Cerny, P. (1995). Globalisation and the changing logic of collective action, *International Organisation*, 49, 4, 595–625.

Cerny, P. (1997). The dynamics of political globalisation, *Government and Opposition*, 32, 2, 251–274.

Christiansen, T. (1996a). A maturing bureaucracy? The role of the Commission in the policy process, in J. Richardson (ed.) *European Union: Power and Policy-making*, London: Routledge, 77–95.

Christiansen, T. (1996b). The European Commission and the legitimacy crisis of European governance, Oslo: European Consortium for Political Research.

Chryssochou, D. (1994). Democracy and symbiosis in the European Union: Towards a confederal consociation?, *West European Politics*, 17, 4, 1–14.

Closa, C. (1996). EU citizenship as the institutional foundation of Union democracy, Oslo: European Consortium for Political Research.

Coase, R. (1960). The problem of social cost, *Journal of Law and Economics*, 3, 1–44.

Cockfield, Lord (1994). *The European Union: Creating the Single Market*, London: Wiley Chancery Law.

Corbett, R., Jacobs, F. and Shackleton, M. (1995). *The European Parliament*, London: Cattermill.

Cullen, D. (1995). Variable geometry and overlapping circles: In search of a suitable model for justice and home affairs, in R. Bieber and J. Monar (eds), *Justice and Home Affairs in the European Union*, Brussels: European University Press.

Dahl, R. (1989). *Democracy and its Critics*, New Haven: Yale University Press.

Davies, N. (1996). *A History of Europe*, Oxford: Oxford University Press.

Dehousse, R. (1995). Institutional reform in the European Community: are there alternatives to the majoritarian avenue?, Florence: EUI Working Paper.

Dehousse, R. (1997). European integration and the nation-state, in M. Rhodes, P. Heywood and V. Wright (eds), *Developments in West European Politics*, Basingstoke: Macmillan. 37–54.

Delors, J. (1994). *L'Unité d'un Homme, Entretiens avec Dominique Wolton*, Paris: Odile Jacob.

De Jong, H. (1995). European capitalism: Between freedom and social justice, *Review of International Economic Organisation*, 10, 399–419.

Deutsch, K., Burrell, S., Kann, R., Lee, M., Lichtermann, M., Loewenheim, F., and Van Wagenen, R. (1957). *Political Community and the North Atlantic Area*, Princeton, NJ: Princeton University Press.

Downs, A. (1957). *An Economic Theory of Democracy*, New York: Harper & Row.

Duchesne, S. and Frognier, A-P. (1995). Is there a European identity, in O. Niedermayer and R. Sinnott (eds), *Public Opinion and International Governance*, Oxford: OUP.

Dyson, K. (1994). *Elusive Union*, London: Longman.

Edwards, G. (1996). National sovereignty vs integration? The Council of Ministers, in J. Richardson (ed.) *European Union: Power and Policy-making*, London: Routledge, 127–47.

Esping-Andersen, G. (1990). *The Three Worlds of Welfare Capitalism*, Princeton, NJ: Princeton University Press.

European Communities (1987). Treaties establishing the European Communities and Documents concerning the Accessions to the European Communities, Luxembourg.

European Communities (1992). The Treaty of European Union, Luxembourg.

European Parliament, Medina Ortega Report, *http://www.europarl.eu.int/ dg1/a4/en/a4-97/a4-0020.*

Europinion (1997). (*http://europa.eu. int*).

Favier, P. and Martin-Roland, M. (1991). *La Décenne Mitterrand 2: Les Épreuves 1984–1988*, Paris: Seuil.

Ferrera, M. (1996). The southern model of welfare in social Europe, *Journal of European Social Policy*, **6**, **1**, 17–37.

Franklin, M. (1996). 'European elections and the European voter', in J. Richardson (ed.), *European Union, Power and Policy Making*, London: Routledge.

Gabel, M. (1994). Balancing democracy and stability: Considering the democratic deficit in the EU from a consociational perspective, Madrid: Paper presented to the ECPR Joint Sessions.

Garrett, G. and Tsebelis, G. (1996). An institutional critique of inter-governmentalism, *International Organisation*, **50**, **2**, 269–99.

Gatsios, K. and Seabright, P. (1989). Regulation in the European Community, *Oxford Review of Economic Policy*, **5**, **2**, 37–60.

Gellner, E. (1983). *Nations and Nationalism*, Oxford: Blackwell.

Gellner, E. (1994). *Civic Society and its Enemies*, Harmonsworth: Penguin.

Giddens, A. (1991). *The Consequences of Modernity*, Cambridge: Polity.

Giddens, A. (1996). *Beyond Left and Right*, Cambridge: Polity.

Graeger, N. (1994). *European Integration and the Legitimation of Supranational Power*, Oslo: Department of Political Science.

Greenwood, J. (1997). *Representing Interests in the European Union*, London: Macmillan.

Gruner, W. (1989). Deutschland und das europäische Gleichgewicht seit dem 18 Jahrhundert, in W. Gruner, *Gleichgewicht in Geschichte und Gegenwart*, Hamburg: 66–133.

Haas, E.B. (1958). *The Uniting of Europe*, Stanford: Stanford University Press.

Habermas, J. (1976). *Legitimation Crisis*, London: Heinemann.

Habermas, J. (1992). Citizenship and national identity: some reflections on the future of Europe, *Praxis International*, **12**, **1**, 1–19.

Habermas, J. (1996). The European nation state – its achievements and its limits. On the past and future of sovereignty and citizenship, *Ratio Juris*, **9**, **2**.

Hall, J. (1985). *Powers and Liberties: the Causes and Consequences of the Rise of the West*, Harmondsworth, Penguin.

Hall, J.A. (1993). Consolidations of democracy, in D. Held (ed.) *Prospects for Democracy*, Cambridge: Polity, 271–90.

Hallstein, W. (1970). *L'Europe Inachevée*, Paris: Robert Laffont.

Harrison, R. (1974). *Europe in Question: Theories of Regional International Integration*, London: Allen and Unwin.

Hayes-Renshaw, F. and Wallace, H. (1996). *The Council of Ministers*, Basingstoke: Macmillan.

Held, D. (ed.) (1993). *Prospects for Democracy: North, South, East and West*, Cambridge: Polity.

Held, D. (1996). *Models of Democracy*, Cambridge: Polity.

Hill, C. (ed.) (1983). *National Foreign Policies and European Political Co-operation*, London: Allen and Unwin.

Hill, C. (1991). The European Community; towards a common foreign and security policy, *World Today*, 47, 11.

Hirst, P. (1997). The global economy – myths and realities, *International Affairs*, 73, 3, 409–27.

Hirst, P. and Thompson, G. (1996). Global myths and national policies, *Renewal*, 4, 2.

Hix, S. (1994). The study of the European Community: the challenge of comparative politics, *West European Politics*, 17, 1, 1–30.

Hix, S. and Lord, C. (1996). The making of a President: The European Parliament and the Confirmation of Jacques Santer as President of the Commission, *Government and Opposition*, 31, 1, 62–76.

Hix, S. and Lord, C. (1997). *Political Parties in the European Union*, Basingstoke: Macmillan.

Hix, S. and Lord, C. (forthcoming) A model transnational party? The party of European Socialists, in D. Bell and C. Lord (eds) (forthcoming) *Transnational Parties in the European Union*, Aldershot: Ashgate.

Hobsbawm, E. (1994). *Age of Extremes. The Short Twentieth Century 1914–91*, London: Abacus.

Hoffman, S. (1966). Obstinate or obsolete? The fate of the nation-state and the case of western Europe, *Daedalus*, 95, 862–915.

Hooghe, L. (1995). Subnational mobilisation in the European Union, *West European Politics*, 18, 3, 175–98.

Howard, M. (1983). *The Causes of Wars*, London: Counterpoint.

Howe, P. (1995). 'A community of Europeans: The requisite underpinnings', *Journal of Common Market Studies*, 33, 1, 27–46.

Howe, P. (1997). 'Insiders and outsiders in a community of Europeans: A reply to Kostakopoulou', *Journal of Common Market Studies*, 35, 2.

Horton, J. (1992). *Political Obligation*, Basingstoke: Macmillan.

Hurrell, A. and Manon, A. (1996). Politics like any other? Comparative politics, international relations and the study of the EU, *West European Politics*, 19, 2, 386–402.

Ifestos, P. (1987). *European Political Co-operation: Towards a Framework of Supranational Diplomacy*, Aldershot: Avebury.

Inglehart, R. (1970). Cognitive mobilisation and European identity, *Comparative Politics*, 3, 1, 45–70.

Inglehart, R. (1977). Long-term trends in mass support for European unification, *Government and Opposition*, 12, 1, 150–77.

Inglehart, R. (1991). Trust between nations: Primordial ties, societal learning and economic development, in R. Inglehart and K. Reif (eds), *Eurobarometer: The Dynamics of European Public Opinion*, Basingstoke: Macmillan.

Inman, R. and Rubinfeld, D. (1997). The political economy of federalism, in D. Mueller (ed.), *Perspectives in Public Choice*, Cambridge: Cambridge University Press.

Jervis, J. (1976). *Perception and Misperception in International Politics*, Princeton, NJ: Princeton University Press.

Judge, D. (1995). The failure of national parliaments?, *West European Politics*, **18**, 3, 79–100.

Kahnemann, D., Slovik, P. and Tversky, A. (eds) (1982). *Judgement under Uncertainty*, London: Cambridge University Press.

Katz, R. and Mair, P. (1995). Changing models of party organisation and party democracy: the emergence of the cartel party, *Party Politics*, **1**, 1, 5–28.

Keohane, R. and Nye, J. (1977). *Power and Interdependence*, Boston, MA: Little, Brown.

Kissinger, H. (1982). *Years of Upheaval*, London: Weidenfeld and Nicholson.

Kohler-Koch, B. (1996). Catching up with change: the transformation of governance in the European Union, *Journal of European Public Policy*, **3**, 3, 359–80.

Kolodziej, E. (1974). *French International Policy under De Gaulle and Pompidou*, Ithaca, NY: Cornell University Press.

Kostakopoulou, T. (1997). Why a 'Community of Europeans' could be a community of exclusion: A reply to Howe, *Journal of Common Market Studies*, **35**, 2, 301–8.

Kydland, F. and Prescott, E. (1977). Rules rather than discretion: the inconsistency of optimal plans, *Journal of Political Economy*, **85**, 3, 137–60.

Laffan, B. (1996). The politics of identity and political order in Europe, *Journal of Common Market Studies*, **34**, 1, 81–103.

Lawson, N. (1992). *The View from No. 11. Memoirs of a Tory Radical*, London: Bantam.

Lijphart, A. (1984). *Democracies: Patterns of Majoritarian and Consensus Government in Twenty-One Countries*, New Haven, CA: Yale University Press.

Lindberg, L. and Scheingold, S. (1970). *Europe's Would-be Polity*, Englewood Cliffs, NY: Prentice Hall.

Lipset, S. (1958). Some social requisites of democracy, *American Political Studies Review*, **53**, 69–105.

Locke, J. (1952). *The Second Treatise of Government*, New York: Bobbs Merrill.

Lodge, J. (1994). Transparency and democratic legitimacy, *Journal of Common Market Studies*, **32**, 3, 81–103.

Lord, C. (1991). From intergovernmental to interparliamentary union, *Contemporary European Affairs*, **4**, 2/3.

Lord, C. (1993). *British entry to the European Community under the Heath Government of 1970–4*, Aldershot: Dartmouth.

Ludlow, P. (1991). The European Commission, in R.O. Keohane and S. Hoffman (eds) *The New European Community: Decision Making and Institutional Change*, Boulder, CO: Westview, 88–132.

Lukes, S. (1974). *Power, A Radical View*, London: Macmillan.

Mair, P. (1994). The correlates of consensus democracy and the puzzle of Dutch politics, *West European Politics*, **17**, 4, 97–123.

Majone, G. (1993). The European Community between social policy and social regulation, *Journal of Common Market Studies*, **31**, 2, 153–70.

Majone, G. (1996). A European regulatory state? in J. Richardson (ed.) (1996) *European Union: Power and Policy Making*, London: Routledge.

Majone, G. (1996) Regulatory legitimacy, in G. Majone (ed.) *Regulating Europe*, London: Routledge, 284–301.

March, J. and Olson, J. (1984). The new institutionalism: Organisational factors in political life, *American Political Science Review*, **78**, 734–49.

Marks, G., Hooghe, L. and Blank, K. (1996). 'European integration from the 1980s: State-centric vs multi-level governance, *Journal of Common Market Studies*, **34**, 3, 341–78.

Mazey, S. and Richardson, J. (eds) (1993). *Lobbying in the European Community*, Oxford: Oxford University Press.

Meehan, E. (1993). *Citizenship and the European Community*, London: Sage.

Miller, D. (1993). Deliberative democracy and social choice', in D. Held, (ed.) *Prospects for Democracy*, Cambridge: Polity.

Milward, A. (1992). *The European Rescue of the Nation State*, London: Routledge.

Mitrany, D. (1943). *A Working Peace System*, Chicago, IL: Quadrangle Books.

Monnet, J. (1976). *Mémoires*, Paris: Fayard.

Moravcsik, A. (1989). Integrating international and domestic theories of international bargaining, in Putnam and Bayne, 3–999.

Moravcsik, A. (1991). 'Negotiating the Single European Act: national interests and conventional statecraft in the European Community', *International Organisation*, 45, 1, 19–56.

Moravcsik, A. (1993). Preferences and power in the European Community: a liberal intergovernmentalist approach, *Journal of Common Market Studies*, **31**, 4, 473–524.

Moravcsik, A. (1993) 'Introduction' in Evans, P., Jacobson, H. and Putnam, R. (eds) Double-edged Diplomacy: International Bargaining and Domestic Politics, Berkeley: University of California Press.

Niedermayer, O. and Sinnott, R. (eds) (1995). *Public Opinion and Internationalized Governance*, Oxford: Oxford University Press.

Norton, P. (ed.) (1996). *National Parliaments and the European Union*, London: Frank Cass.

Nozick, R. (1974). *Anarchy, State and Utopia*, Oxford: Blackwell.

Obradovic, D. (1996). Policy legitimacy and the European Union, *Journal of Common Market Studies*, 34, 2, 191–221.

Olson, M. (1965). *The Logic of Collective Action: Public Goods and the Theory of Groups*, Cambridge, MA: Cambridge University Press.

Ostrom, E. and Walker, J. (1997). Neither markets nor states: Linking transformation processes in collective action arenas, in D. Mueller (ed.), *Perspectives on Public Choice*, Cambridge: Cambridge University Press, 35–72.

Pateman, C. (1985). *The Problem of Political Obligation*, Cambridge: Polity.

Peters, B.G. (1994). Agenda setting in the European Community, *Journal of European Public Policy*, 1, 1, 9–26.

Peters, B.G. (1996). Agenda-setting in the European Union, in J. Richardson (ed.) *European Union: Power and Policy Making*, 61–76.

Peterson, J. (1995). Decision making in the European Union: towards a framework for analysis, *Journal of European Public Policy*, 2, 1, 69–93.

Peterson, J. (1997). The European Union: Pooled sovereignty, divided accountability, *Political Studies*, 45, 3, 559–79.

Plamenatz, J. (1973). *Democracy and Illusion: An examination of certain aspects of modern democratic theory*, London: Longman.

Plato (1961). *The Statesman*, J.B. Skemp (ed.), London: Routledge Kegan Paul.

Plato (1976). *Protagoras*, C.C.W. Taylor (ed.), Oxford: Clarendon Press.

Poidevin, R. (1986). *Robert Schuman: Homme D'État*, Paris: Imprimerie Nationale.

Pollack, M. (1997). Delegation, agency and agenda setting in the European Community, *International Organisation*, 51, 1, 99–134.

Reif, H. and Schmitt, H. (1980). Nine second-order national elections: A conceptual framework for the analysis of European election results, *European Journal of Political Research*, 8, 1, 3–44.

Rengger, N. (1997). The ethics of trust in world politics, *International Affairs*, 73, 3, 469–88.

Rhodes, M. (1997). The welfare state: Internal challenges, external constraints, in M. Rhodes, P. Heywood and V. Wright (eds), *Developments in West European Politics*, Basingstoke: Macmillan.

Richardson, J. (ed.) (1996). *European Union: Power and Policy Making*, London: Routledge.

Risse-Kappen, T. (1996). Exploring the nature of the beast: international relations theory and comparative policy analysis meet in the European Union, *Journal of Common Market Studies*, 34, 1, 53–80.

Roberts, J.M. (ed.) (1966). *French Revolution Documents*, Vol. 1, Oxford: Blackwell.

Ross, G. (1995). *Jacques Delors and European Integration*, Cambridge: Polity.

Rousseau, J-J. (1963). *The Social Contract and Discourses*, London: Dent.

Sandholtz, W. (1996). Membership matters: Limits of the functional approach to European institutions, *Journal of Common Market Studies*, **34**, 3, 403–29.

Sartori, G. (1988). *The Theory of Democracy Revisited*, Chatham, NJ: Chatham House.

Sbragia, A. (1996). Environmental policy, in H. Wallace and W. Wallace (eds), *Policy-Making in the European Union*, Oxford: OUP.

Schaar, J.H. (1984). Legitimacy in the modern state, in W. Connolly (ed.) *Legitimacy and the State*, Oxford: Blackwell, 104–33.

Scharpf, F. (1988). The joint decision trap: lessons from German federalism and European integration, *Public Administration*, **66**, 3.

Scharpf, F. (1997). Economic integration, democracy and the welfare state, *Journal of European Public Policy*, **4**, 1, 18–36.

Schattsneider, E.E. (1960). *The semi-sovereign people. A realist's view of democracy in America*, New York: Holt.

Schmidt, V. (1997). European integration and democracy: the differences among member states, *Journal of European Public Policy*, **4**, 1, 128–45.

Schmitter, P. (1971). 'A revised theory of regional integration' in L.N. Lindberg and S.A. Scheingold (eds), *Regional Integration: Theory and Research*, Cambridge, MA: Harvard University Press.

Schmitter, P. (1995). Alternatives for the future European polity: Is federalism the only answer? in M. Telò, *Démocratie et la Construction Européenne*, Bruxelles: Editions de l'Université de Bruxelles.

Schmitter, P. (1996). Is it really possible to democratise the Euro-polity?, Oslo: European Consortium for Political Research.

Scholte, J-A. (1997). Global capitalism and the state, *International Affairs*, **73**, 3, 427–53.

Schumpeter, J. (1943). *Capitalism, Socialism and Democracy*, London: Allen and Unwin.

Sebenius, J. (1992). Challenging conventional explanations of international co-operation: Negotiation analysis and the case of epistemic communities, *International Organisation*, **46**, 1, 323–65.

Shepsle, K. (1989). Studying institutions: Some lessons from the rational choice approach, *Journal of Theoretical Politics*, **1**, 2, 131–47.

Simon, H. (1983). *Reason in Human Affairs*, Oxford: Blackwell.

Smith, A. (1991). *National Identity*, London: Penguin.

Smith, A.D. (1992). National identity and the idea of European unity, *International Affairs*, **68**, 1, 55–76.

Smith, M. (1996). 'The EU as an international actor', in J. Richardson (ed.) *European Union: Power and Policy Making*, London: Routledge.

Steinbruner, J. (1974). *The Cybernetic Theory of Decision,* Princeton, NJ: Princeton University Press.

Storey, H. (1995). Human rights and the new Europe: experience and experiment, in D. Beetham (ed.) *Politics and Human Rights,* Oxford: Blackwell, 131–51.

Stubb, A. (1996). A categorisation of differentiated integration, *Journal of Common Market Studies,* 34, 2.

Taylor, P. (1983). *The Limits of European Integration,* London: Croom Helm.

Taylor, P. (1991). *International Organization in the Modern World: The Regional and the Global Process,* London: Pinter.

Taylor, P. (1993). *International Organisation in the Modern World: The Regional and the Global Process,* London: Pinter.

Teasdale, A. (1993). The life and death of the Luxembourg compromise, *Journal of Common Market Studies,* 31, 4, 567–79.

Telò, M. (1995). *Démocratie et Construction Européenne,* Bruxelles: Université Libre de Bruxelles.

Thomson, D. (1969). *Democracy in France since 1870,* London: Oxford University Press.

Touraine, A. (1994). *Qu'est-ce que la démocratie?,* Paris: Librairie Arthème Fayard.

Tranholm-Mikkelsen, J. (1991). Neofunctionalism: obstinate or obsolete? A reappraisal in the light of the new dynamism of the EC, *Millennium,* 20, 1, 1–22.

Treaty establishing the European Coal and Steel Community, 18 April 1951, *http://europa. eu. int/abc/obj/treaties.*

Treaty Establishing the European Community, 25 March 1957, *http://europa.eu. int/abc/obj/treaties.*

Tsebelis, G. (1990). *Nested Games,* Berkeley: University of California Press.

Tsoukalis, L. and Rhodes, M. (1997). Economic integration and the nation state, in M. Rhodes, P. Heywood and V. Wright (eds), *Developments in West European Politics,* Basingstoke: Macmillan.

Wagner, H. (1993). 'Constitutional patriotism' as an antidote, *Aussenpolitik,* 44, 3, 243–52.

Walker, G.E. (ed.) (1841). *Presidents' Messages,* New York: Walker.

Wallace, H. (1993). Deepening and widening: problems of legitimacy for the EC, in S. Garcia (ed.) *European Identity and the Search for Legitimacy,* London: Pinter, 95–105.

Wallace, H. (ed.) (1991). *The Wider Western Europe: Reshaping the EC/ EFTA Relationship,* London: RIIA/Pinter.

Wallace, H. and Ridley, A. (1985). *Europe: The Challenge of Diversity,* London: RIIA/RKP.

Wallace, H. and Wallace, W. (eds) (1996). *Policy Making in the European Union,* London: Oxford University Press.

Wallace, H. and Wessels, W. (1991). Introduction, in H. Wallace (ed.) *The Wider Western Europe: Reshaping the EC/EFTA Relationship*, London: Pinter/RIIA.

Wallace, W. (1990). *The Transformation of Western Europe*, London: Pinter.

Wallace, W. and Smith, J. (1995). Democracy or technocracy? European integration and the problem of popular consent, *West European Politics*, **18**, 3, 137–57.

Waltz, K. (1979). *Theory of International Relations*, Cambridge, MA: Addison Wesley.

Weale, A. (1998). Between representation and constitutionalism in the European Union (forthcoming) in M. Nentwich and A. Weale (eds), *The Political Theory of European Constitutional Choice*, London: Routledge.

Weber, M. (1978). *Economy and Society*, Berkeley, CA: University of California Press.

Weidenfeld, W. (1994). *Europa '96 Reformprogramm für die Europäische Union*, Gütersloh: Bertelsmann.

Weiler, J.H.H. (1992). After Maastricht: Community legitimacy in post-1992 Europe, in W.J. Adams (ed.) *Singular Europe: Economy and Polity of the European Community after 1992*, Ann Arbor, MF: University of Michigan Press, 11–41.

Weiler, J., Haltern, U. and Mayer, F. (1995). 'European democracy and its critique', *West European Politics*, **18**, 3, 4–39.

Weiler, J. (1997a). The reformation of European constitutionalism, *Journal of Common Market Studies*, **35**, 1, 97–131.

Weiler, J. (1997b). Legitimacy and democracy of Union governance, in G. Edwards and A. Pijpers (eds) *The Politics of European Union Treaty Reform*, London: Pinter.

Welsh, J.M. (1993). A people's Europe? European citizenship and European identity, *Politics*, **13**, 2, 25–31.

Wessels, W. Staat und (westeuropaische) Integration: die Fusionsthese, *Politische Vierteljarhresschift*, Sonderheft **23**, 99, 36–61.

Wessels, W. (1997). 'A dynamic macropolitical view on integration processes', *Journal of Common Market Studies*, **35**, 2, 267–99.

Williams, S. (1991). Sovereignty and accountability in the European community, in R.O. Keohane and S. Hoffmann (eds) *The New European Community: Decision Making and Institutional Change*, Boulder, CO: Westview, 153–76.

Williamson, O. (1985). *The Economic Institutions of Capitalism*, New York: Free Press.

Zetterholm, S. (ed.) (1994). *National Cultures and European Integration*, Oxford: Berg.

Index

141